finding
PEACE

finding
PEACE

compiled by

SISTER STAN

First published in 2021 by

 columba BOOKS

Block 3b, Bracken Business Park,
Bracken Road, Sandyford, Dublin 18, D18 K277
www.columbabooks.com

ISBN: 978-1-78218-381-5

Set in FreightDisp Pro 11/15 and Essonnes Display
Book and cover design by Alba Esteban | Columba Books
Illustrations by @coolvector | Freepik
Printed with L&C, Poland

* * *

To Patrick and Gladys Lydon for their lifelong
inspirational dedicated service in Camphill.

* * *

* * *

"And I shall have some peace there,
for peace comes dropping slow,
Dropping from the veils of the morning
to where the cricket sings;
There midnight's all a glimmer, and noon a purple glow,
And evening full of the linnet's wings."

William Butler Yeats,
The Lake Isle of Innisfree

* * *

TABLE OF CONTENTS

PEACE

There is only silence
On the mountain tops
Among the tips of the trees
You perceive barely a breath
Even the birds in the forest
Keep still and are silent
Wait then
Just a little while longer
And you too
Will find peace at last.

J.W. von Goethe

INTRODUCTION

· · · · · · · · · · · · · · · · · ·

I have had cause recently, for various reasons – including the restrictions imposed during the Covid-19 pandemic – to live a quieter and more solitary life than I had done previously. I found this change from a more hectic lifestyle brought me great benefits. It gave me a chance to pause, to step back and to let go of things that I had thought were important, but which turned out not to be so important after all. It was a challenging time, but it was also a rewarding time, a time of opening up to an inner world.

I came to rely more and more on my own inner resources. I prayed more and I meditated more. I sat with silence more and tried, in so far as I could, to let inner peace find me. I read poems, over and over again, and I found that the poems I read were calling me to rest in my inner life. John Donohue put it like this: 'Gradually, you will return to yourself, having learned a new respect for your heart, And the joy that dwells far within slow time.'

I was drawn to writings on peace by well-known, and some not so well-known, people in the past. I collected them, collated them and meditated on them. It was that experience of trying to find my own way to a more peaceful life that made me wonder about the journeys that other people make today in their daily lives towards inner peace, and I thought it would be interesting to find out about that. And that is how this book began.

I asked all the contributors to this book the same question: 'Where and how do you find peace in your daily life?' The people I asked this question of are all highly regarded in their own field. They represent a broad spectrum of Irish life.

Even as I wrote my letters asking people for their contributions, I knew this was not an easy request that I was making. As people came back to me to talk about what I had asked of them, I became even more aware of how difficult a question I had posed. Many were resistant to the idea of disclosing such a deeply private matter. However, as the responses came in, my apprehensions disappeared. What people wrote amounted to an outpouring of honesty. I could tell that these responses were authentic, because they were so definite and so personal.

Every response was unique – every individual had something different to offer – and so the material here is diverse and wide-ranging. Some people told me that they found peace in their daily life with their family and friends; others found it in meditation and prayer; many found it in the natural world; and others again in music. But wherever and however they found it, all the contributions were a testament to an inner life that needs to be sustained, especially in times of crisis. I could see from what people told me that there is a human need for something beyond the routine and materialism of everyday life.

I found all the contributions in their own way led me to a greater inner peace myself.

This book offers serious and interesting insights into people's lives. I am sure the contributors all found, as I did, that in trying to write about peace, the writing itself reveals ourselves to ourselves, a process that is in constant evolution.

For me, this short poem by Michael Leunig helped me on my quest for peace:

God help us to live slowly:
To move simply:
To look softly:
To allow emptiness:
To let the heart create for us.
Amen.

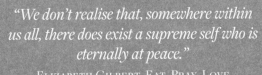

"We don't realise that, somewhere within us all, there does exist a supreme self who is eternally at peace."

ELIZABETH GILBERT, EAT, PRAY, LOVE

* * *

"'When you search for me, you will find me. If you seek me with all your heart I will let you find me,' says the Lord."

JEREMIAH 29:13

* * *

"To set the mind on the flesh is death, but to set the mind on the Spirit is life and peace."

ROMANS 8:6

PEACE COMES DROPPING SLOW

Mark Patrick Hederman

I f I am agitated and want to find peace, I imagine myself in a beautiful place, usually on a beach or in a meadow where I have felt happy once. In my mind I get myself to lie down there, leaving above me like a mist of swirling insects, whatever is bothering my mind. I imagine that all those things which are worrying me are in two large rucksacks which I take off my shoulders and lay down at some distance. I imagine myself in the valley of dry bones visited by Ezekiel. Each of my limbs is laid out in the grass or on the sand as part of that vast company of dry bones.

I use my mind as an internal soother with which to visit each joint and limb of my extended body, starting with my toes and moving upward. Carefully concentrating, naming, and feeling each one, I visit and caress them, gently urging them to relax. Coming up through my ankles, my knees, my stomach, my chest, my shoulders, my neck and eventually massaging inwardly the top of my scalp, I allow the assorted pieces to chill out as if they didn't belong to each other.

Once every one of these portions of my body have been quietened, I invite the Holy Spirit like a gentle breeze to circulate and refresh what has now become a series of items laid out on grass or sand. No longer a scrunched up mass of seething tension, the gentle breeze visits the spaces between each one of my limbs and releases that tension that makes them cling together. Such distribution on sand or grass relaxes me and allows me to become aware of the beauty that surrounds me, and which can now permeate what was, minutes before, impenetrable.

I am now able to engage with the elements. The sun touching my skin, the earth warming my body, the sounds from insects and birds caressing my ears, the scents that seep through my nostrils encourage me to breathe deeply and welcome the fresh air right down as far as the pit of my stomach. This breathing in and out is a Eucharist: thanksgiving and blessing for the universe. Relaxing the muscles around my eyes, especially where the forehead is clenched into a fist, my gaze can wander freely across the vast friendliness of the open sky. I end up as if I were asleep but without losing consciousness. My worries and concerns lose their particularity and purchase. They rise like vapours towards another dimension where they lose their impact. I am at peace.

. . . .

Mark Patrick Hederman OSB is a Benedictine monk, teacher, lecturer and writer based in Glenstal Abbey, Co. Limerick.

"If you cannot find peace within yourself, you will never find it anywhere else."

MARVIN GAYE, AMERICAN SINGER-SONGWRITER

* * *

"O Lord, you have searched me and you know me. You know when I sit and when I rise; you perceive my thoughts from afar. You discern my going out and my lying down; you are familiar with all my ways."

PSALM 139: 1-3

PEACE BEGINS WITH A SMILE

Miriam O'Callaghan

Many of you might recognise that my title is a quote from Mother Teresa. I have always loved it and try to practice it a lot in my own life. Peace means different things to all of us of course, but for me it's really just a state of mind, anchored in happiness and gratitude.

I am lucky to have a very busy family life. I love it and feel eternally grateful for it. The noise, chat, laughter, a home full of energy, provide the wonderful backdrop to my life. My Mum has always described my house as 'a little like Heuston Station at its busiest.' Down the years, with eight children and their many friends popping in and out, plus our two dogs, my husband Steve and I often laugh together that we can only ever dream of solitude. I would not like it any other way. How do you survive though with so little peace, I am often asked, but I realise that my idea of peace is perhaps different to others. My peace is being happy. Waking up every day and knowing that my family right now are all healthy and happy, never ever taking that for granted, and being always grateful for that good fortune.

I think losing my precious sister Anne to cancer when she was just 33 years of age made me realise just how fragile life is, how important it is to realise that, and to not waste my time planning what I might be doing tomorrow or next week or even next year, instead of focusing all my energies on living for today, living in the moment and enjoying it. That is how I live my life on a daily basis – grateful, happy and smiling as much as I can. That is my peace.

When John Lennon was five years of age his mother told him that happiness was the key to life. So when he went to school, the teacher asked him what he wanted to be when he grew up. He wrote down "happy". He was told that he didn't understand the assignment – he told the teacher they didn't understand life. I agree with John's mum. Happiness is the key to life. My peace is knowing that.

* *

Miriam O' Callaghan is a television and radio presenter.

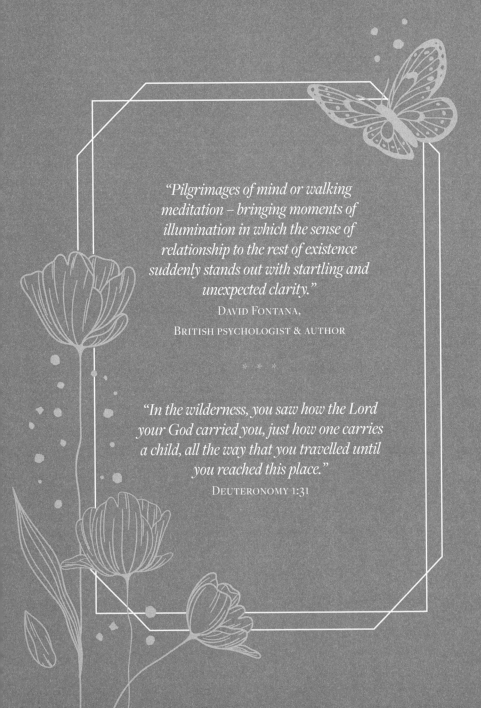

"Pilgrimages of mind or walking
meditation – bringing moments of
illumination in which the sense of
relationship to the rest of existence
suddenly stands out with startling and
unexpected clarity."

DAVID FONTANA,
BRITISH PSYCHOLOGIST & AUTHOR

* * *

"In the wilderness, you saw how the Lord
your God carried you, just how one carries
a child, all the way that you travelled until
you reached this place."

DEUTERONOMY 1:31

TREASURED MOMENTS

. . . .

Johnny Sexton

P eace comes and goes in my life.
    There is a part of me that is always at peace but sometimes I need to take time to seek it out.

In my preparation for sport, I place a significant emphasis on the importance of meditation, which touches into peace.

In big games when the adrenalin is in full flow and I prepare to take an important kick, I have learned how to breathe deeply and enter into a moment of pure concentration and calm. The stadium goes silent and it is a special, and I would say peaceful, moment.

When I am faced with a difficult challenge or problem, I find a long walk or a run very effective in giving me the time and perspective to work these through to resolution.

At home, Laura and I have three young children so our house is regularly busy and loud. I really enjoy spending time with the children and immersing myself in their world – this is my ultimate de-stressing tool!

. . . .

Johnny Sexton is a professional rugby player who plays for Leinster, Ireland and the British & Irish Lions. He is married to Laura and dad to Luca, Amy and Sophie.

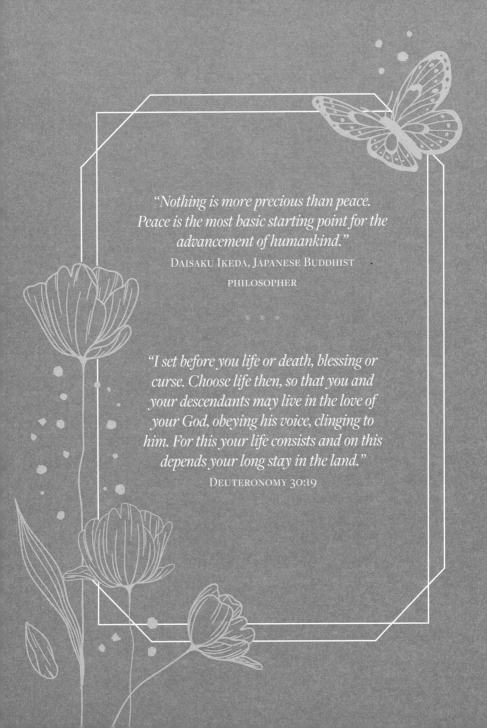

"*Nothing is more precious than peace. Peace is the most basic starting point for the advancement of humankind.*"

DAISAKU IKEDA, JAPANESE BUDDHIST PHILOSOPHER

* * *

"*I set before you life or death, blessing or curse. Choose life then, so that you and your descendants may live in the love of your God, obeying his voice, clinging to him. For this your life consists and on this depends your long stay in the land.*"

DEUTERONOMY 30:19

PENCIL PEACE

· · · · · · · · · · · · · · · · · · ·

Emily O'Reilly

I have, what yoga instructors call a 'monkey' mind, constantly leaping about so that even my downtime is never quite that.

In the summer of 2019, I spent a week at the Burren College of Art taking classes in botanical drawing to calm me down before my re-election campaign for European Ombudsman. I had anticipated Zen; what I got was severe stress on day three when I observed the wreckage on the pages before me. I slunk away ashamed, an afternoon early.

Then came the Covid-19 lockdown. Work migrated to a small physical space. The monkey mind was swinging from the rafters. I reached for the pencils.

Drawing became my time of peace at close of day, when the monkeys sat quietly, soundlessly, on their branches and nothing intruded. The mastery proved to be not of the skill itself – that takes lightyears that I do not have – but of the compulsion to rush, to finish, to produce, to display.

To find that peace, I had to learn to put my mind into slow motion, not to scribble but to think and plan and take time over the tiniest detail. I had to learn to master the satisfaction of the process, not the product.

I read of botanical artists who take weeks or months to complete the smallest but most exquisite of drawings. In time I learned to be happy with just a single vein that came to a rational halt as it curved through the filigree of an extraordinary leaf system.

I reduced my ambition to an accurate petiole and no longer to a thumping great vase of blowsy lilies, to a showpiece that would in any event end in tears.

All my monkey mind had needed to be still was an HB pencil, humility and an exceedingly good eraser.

· ·

Emily O'Reilly is the European Ombudsman and the former Irish Ombudsman and Information Commissioner. Prior to those appointments she was a journalist and author. She is married with five children and currently lives in Strasbourg, France.

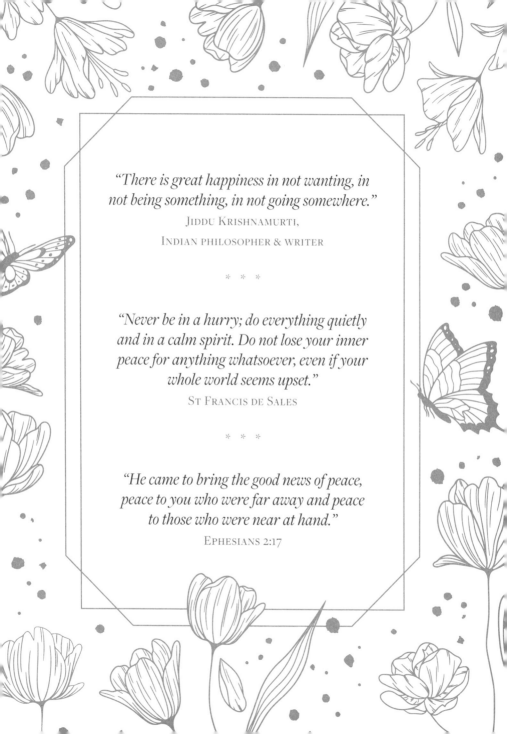

"*There is great happiness in not wanting, in not being something, in not going somewhere.*"

JIDDU KRISHNAMURTI,
INDIAN PHILOSOPHER & WRITER

* * *

"*Never be in a hurry; do everything quietly and in a calm spirit. Do not lose your inner peace for anything whatsoever, even if your whole world seems upset.*"

ST FRANCIS DE SALES

* * *

"*He came to bring the good news of peace, peace to you who were far away and peace to those who were near at hand.*"

EPHESIANS 2:17

BELOW DREAMING

· ·

Tommy Tiernan

There'll be peace enough when you die. Life maybe is too overwhelming, too immersive and challenging to ever be peaceful. The Christian adventure is sometimes presented as a journey. From sinner to saint at its most extreme but perhaps more ordinarily from the Garden of Eden to...I don't know, somewhere paradisal like back to the Garden of Eden. The journey to where you are, I suppose. And journeys involve effort and movement, through 'hollow lands and hilly lands', through countless winters and springs, peoples and places. All the time, moving. And while there may be moments of peace, an afternoon, a week, it's not something that happens too often and we shouldn't think of its absence as a fault. In the same way that acute stress isn't a constant, peace isn't there all the time either.

Any attempt to define life is always frustrating because the experience of being alive is always larger than language. This is why we love stories so much. A story can hint or point or testify to something without trying to classify it. And a good story will raise more questions than it answers. The one that I have in mind at the moment is Christ at The Last Supper.

That Thursday evening was the beginning of the chaos. They were being hunted, they would never sit like this again. The unity of the group was about to be shattered, their leader, the head of the family about to be murdered, betrayed by one of them. And in the midst of all this he turns to them and says:

'I leave you peace, my peace I give you.'

What did he mean?

We're free from all trouble in dreamless sleep. Like we were before we were conceived. And death may well be the same, although it's hardly what you would call an 'experience'. Every night when we sink below dreaming we get peace. A few hours of it. We register nothing, we're conscious of nothing. But as soon as we open our eyes we plunge again into the overwhelming, topsy turvy world of the senses. Let us try and fully participate in that while we have the chance.

Tommy Tiernan is a comedian, actor, writer and presenter.

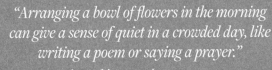

"Arranging a bowl of flowers in the morning can give a sense of quiet in a crowded day, like writing a poem or saying a prayer."

ANNE MORROW LINDBERGH,
AMERICAN AUTHOR & AVIATOR

* * *

"Observe the wonders as they occur around you. Don't claim them. Feel the artistry moving through and be silent. Don't grieve. Anything you lose comes round in another form."

RUMI, PERSIAN POET & SUFI MYSTIC

* * *

"May Yahweh uncover his face to you and bring you peace."

NUMBERS 6:26

FINDING PEACE IN NATURE

Vicky Phelan

How I find peace in my daily life starts with the same ritual every morning. Before I even get out of bed to start my day, I do a quick assessment of my body for any new aches and pains. When I realise that I am in good shape, I thank the universe for my good health and start the day as I mean to go on, being grateful to be alive and well and to be given more time with my family and friends. This ritual helps me to face the day with a positive mindset, regardless of what the weather is like outside or what is facing me that day.

For me, being in nature is where I find peace. Every day without fail, unless I am very ill, I make sure that I spend time in nature. I go for a walk and I take the time to really enjoy nature, free from any interruptions from phones or electronic devices. I look at the sky, I listen to the birds, I watch the trees sway in the wind and I quieten my mind.

Autumn is a particularly favourite time of the year for me with all the beautiful colours of the trees on display. My absolute favourite sound though, is the sound of the water. I love the sea and when I can't get to it, I have recordings of the sound of the waves at my favourite beach and I play it whenever I need to find a bit of peace.

Vicky Phelan is a women's health advocate and CervicalCheck campaigner. In 2011 she participated in the national cervical screening programme. Her test results were wrongly reported as normal, a fact that was withheld from her, and just two years later she developed cervical cancer. She took the decision to make public her experience and expose the screening programme and the healthcare system to much-needed examination, something which is ongoing.

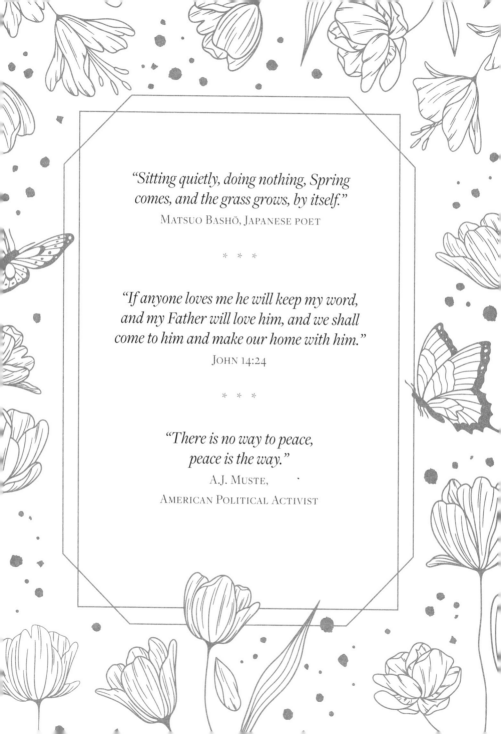

"*Sitting quietly, doing nothing, Spring comes, and the grass grows, by itself.*"

MATSUO BASHŌ, JAPANESE POET

* * *

"*If anyone loves me he will keep my word, and my Father will love him, and we shall come to him and make our home with him.*"

JOHN 14:24

* * *

"*There is no way to peace, peace is the way.*"

A.J. MUSTE,
AMERICAN POLITICAL ACTIVIST

THE ARMCHAIR OF PEACE

Alan Hilliard

I t's an armchair, an old one and part of a set that my mother bought when she won the Mater Hospital Pools in nineteen-sixty something. Previous to that the sitting room was locked and bare. The win allowed her to furnish the empty space with carpet, curtains and furniture.

One of these armchairs is now by my patio door. It is where I sit in the morning to delve into life, prayer and, more often than not, God delves into me. The armchair reminds me that this is a different place; I'm not watching telly, not gazing into the food press, not reading the paper or looking into a laptop. It is different because it is a place that is distinctive to most other things throughout the day. The whole purpose of the armchair is to sit in it and do nothing – at least it can appear to be like that and more often enough it can feel like that too! At the start of my day it reminds me to sit and to do nothing with God, and when I eventually get comfortable He uses the space of nothingness to whisper His words to me. Sometimes I hear the click of the kettle as it turns off – I make the pot of tea later.

On the arms of the armchair are my *Book of Psalms* called the *Psalter*. The Psalms carry every human emotion within their word and verse.

God uses them to tell me how I am – sometimes I am reminded I've little to worry about and at other times all that I have to worry about is laid out in front of me. The invitation to 'Come worship the Lord' (Psalm 95) in that armchair is a journey into the soul, the life it gives expression to, and the support of God in that journey. It is not a means of escape. If it is, well then, our prayer is worthless to us, to God and to the human family. The journey to peace is a journey through reality, not away from it.

• •

Alan Hilliard is a priest of the Archdiocese of Dublin and is the Coordinator of the Pastoral Care and Chaplaincy Service at TU Dublin. He is a regular contributor to RTÉ Radio's A Living Word *and is regular contributor to* The Messenger *magazine and is author of a number of books including* Dipping into Lent, Dipping into Advent *and* Dipping into Life.

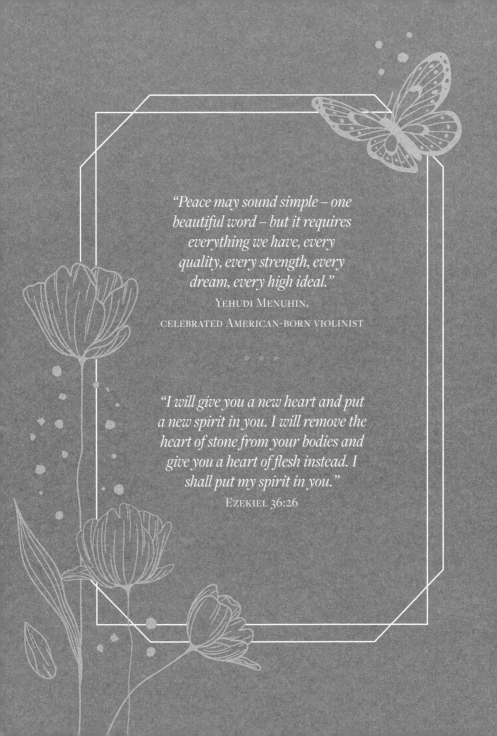

"Peace may sound simple – one beautiful word – but it requires everything we have, every quality, every strength, every dream, every high ideal."

YEHUDI MENUHIN,
CELEBRATED AMERICAN-BORN VIOLINIST

* * *

"I will give you a new heart and put a new spirit in you. I will remove the heart of stone from your bodies and give you a heart of flesh instead. I shall put my spirit in you."

EZEKIEL 36:26

GIVING MY HEAD PEACE

Mary McAleese

I learnt early about the need to find space for peace in my everyday life. My mother regularly referred to the need to get her 'head showered' which means the same thing and has something to do with staying sane and finding the energy to get through the drudgery or messiness of life, while raising nine clamouring children and sundry dogs in a war zone. She found peace and an escape in going to the cinema once a week with her friend Rita, who also had a tribe of children. Back then, as the eldest of the clan, I found my peace locked in the bathroom or hidden down the bottom of the garden reading a book 'in peace'.

In my thirties, and with my own children and a busy career, I took up the practice of meditation, which has been my go to daily peace place for over 30 years. Usually I meditate for 10 minutes a couple of times a day in a quiet room or if the weather is even half reasonable and I have time, I will go for a long walk and meditate; it could be along the Liffey in the centre of Dublin or along the banks of the Shannon in North Roscommon. There, flowing water seems to help clear my head of whatever has colonised it that week.

But more and more during the COVID days, with time to spare, I found peace in music; not thrumming noisy music, but the elegant voices from the past of Jussi Bjorling or Lucia Popp or the great orchestras playing Bach, Chopin, Mahler, Mascagni, Morricone, Rodrigo or Iarlath O'Lionard singling Eleanor Plunkett, or Liam O Flynn piping An Droichead. And I am glad of the gift of hearing that, unfortunately not all are blessed to have, for without beautiful music peace would be hard to find some days.

* *

Mary McAleese is an Irish politician who served as the eighth President of Ireland from 1997 to 2011. She is an award-winning Catholic academic and author, and holds a licentiate and doctorate in Canon law.

"Nobody can bring you peace but yourself."
RALPH WALDO EMERSON,
AMERICAN PHILOSOPHER

* * *

*"It was you who created my innermost
self, put me together in my mother's womb,
for all these mysteries I thank you, for the
wonder of myself, for the wonder of my
works. You know me through and through,
from having watched my bones take shape
when I was being formed in secret, knitted
together in the limbo of the womb."*
PSALM 139:13-16

FINDING PEACE ON THE JOURNEY

Constantine Cavafy

There is a lovely poem called 'Ithaka' by the Greek poet Constantine Cavafy. In it he alludes to the legendary journey of Ulysses as the journey of every person through life. In the end, it is not the goal but the journey that matters, because this journey gives us experience, knowledge and adventure. Here is an extract:

'As you set out for Ithaka
hope the voyage is a long one,
full of adventure, full of discovery.

Keep Ithaka always in your mind.
Arriving there is what you are destined for.
But do not hurry the journey at all.

Better if it lasts for years,
so you are old by the time you reach the island,
wealthy with all you have gained on the way,
not expecting Ithaka to make you rich.

Ithaka gave you the marvellous journey.
Without her you would not have set out.'

. . . .

*Constantine Peter Cavafy was a journalist and
civil servant, and is widely considered the most
distinguished Greek* poet *of the 20th century.*

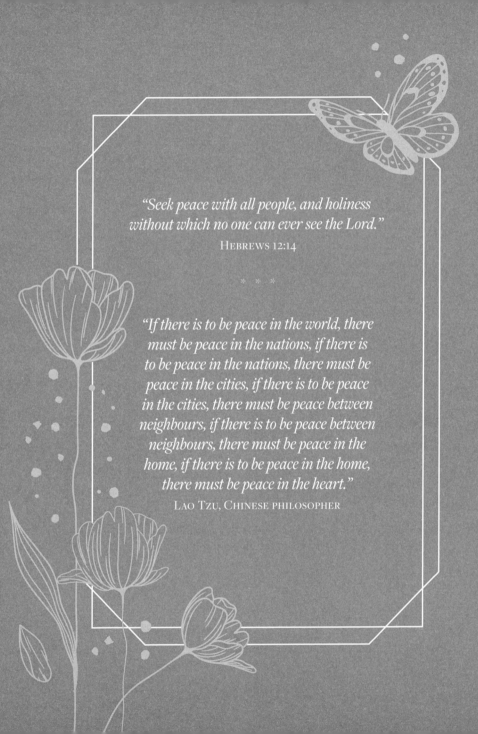

"Seek peace with all people, and holiness without which no one can ever see the Lord."

HEBREWS 12:14

* * *

"If there is to be peace in the world, there must be peace in the nations, if there is to be peace in the nations, there must be peace in the cities, if there is to be peace in the cities, there must be peace between neighbours, if there is to be peace between neighbours, there must be peace in the home, if there is to be peace in the home, there must be peace in the heart."

LAO TZU, CHINESE PHILOSOPHER

MY JOURNEY

· · · · · · · · · · · · · · · ·

Ann Ennis

I t was Friday, 7th June, 2019. A warm sunny morning and I was heading to court for my sentencing. My journey starts here. I was a nervous wreck sitting listening in court, not sure what was happening. The court officer said it was time for me to go to the holding cell. At around 6.30pm an officer collected me and put me into a van. All the way up I cried and I tried to calculate how long would I be away from my family and friends, and my life as I knew it.

When I arrived, the ACO [Assistant Chief Officer] met me and checked me in. Oh my God, my first strip search and I cried and cried. Then up to healthcare. It was horrible. I cried all night thinking I would be in this cell for five years. The cell was very dark and smelly. It had not been painted for years.

Saturday morning came and an officer moved me to a privileged house in the big yard. When I walked across the big yard with the officer, all the women stared at me. I could feel all the women's eyes burning in the back of my head. The women looked normal in my eyes, but some looked rough. I was given a room to myself. Another dark, cold room but at least the walls were better than healthcare. I was delighted because I love time to myself even at home.

A couple of weeks passed and I was working in the kitchen, but I was being bullied. Five weeks later I was still crying, missing home and my normal routine. I was moved again after being beaten up, to a much nicer privileged house. This house was great. If you did not want to go to the yard, you did not have to.

In September I registered for school. The bullying continued and led to me losing my job in the kitchen. This turned out to be a blessing in disguise. A turning point was school and choosing my classes. I joined the Irish Red Cross and threw myself into that. I really liked school, but I think being in the Red Cross was great for me. Bridget, our teacher, was amazing and a great listener.

I did a lot of projects and events. One project that sticks in my mind was called Period Poverty. I was both amazed and disgusted with my findings. In the year 2019/2020 the women in prison were using socks or toilet tissue for sanitary products. This was happening for several reasons:

- Sanitary products were not available in the tuck shop.
- They were too embarrassed to ask for them.
- Female officers only gave 4/5 products, which was not enough as a woman's cycle lasts between 5 to 7 days.
- Older women would never ask for products. The topic of periods was never discussed when they were growing up.
- I also found out that male officers would give more than female officers.

June came and I had my interview for the Outlook Programme with a lady called Ann Kavanagh. We had a great chat about what the programme was all about. I got the news that I was accepted and I would be leaving the Dóchas Centre soon. I could not believe my luck, nothing good ever happens to me. The chief pulled me aside in the yard and congratulated me saying I deserved it because I worked very hard for the programme and I used my time wisely. I felt so happy, happier than I had been in over a year.

I left the Dóchas Centre on July 1st, 2020 and arrived at Stanhope Green. Everybody was so friendly and could not do enough for me. Since leaving the Dóchas Centre I have continued my education in the Pathways Centre. I got a CE [Community Employment] programme placement there and I love going. Everybody is so nice and super friendly.

These days I find peace and happiness in knowing that both my mother and my children are happy and safe. My mother is doing well and I can pick up the phone for a chat anytime. My daughter is an amazing, beautiful young lady, now building a good life for herself. My son has turned his life around after a few bad years. He has a house, a job and a brilliant girl in his life. I have a beautiful grandson who is the apple of my eye and is growing into a very happy, intelligent young lad. I try not to dwell too much on the past, keeping myself busy doing things that I enjoy. I have taken up writing and am continuing in education. Life is good and I am very content.

* *

Ann Ennis is part of the Outlook Programme in Stanhope Green, Dublin which is a joint initiative of the prison service, probation service and Focus Ireland, providing women focussed services to help reduce female offending and improve opportunities for women to reintegrate into their families and communities.

"There are always flowers for those who want to see them."

HENRI MATISSE, FRENCH ARTIST

* * *

"By its nature, hate destroys and tears down, by its very nature, love builds and transforms with redemptive power."

MARTIN LUTHER KING JR, AMERICAN BAPTIST MINISTER AND ACTIVIST

* * *

"And Jacob awoke from his sleep and he said, 'Surely the Lord is in this place and I did not know it.'"

GENESIS 28:16

SURRENDER

· · · · · · · · · · · · · · · ·

Luka Bloom

P eace. It is a great little word, in fairness. Like Love.
Often they come together. Peace and Love.
I want peace.
I want it everywhere.

Peace of mind is the greatest gift of all.
But it can seem like a luxury item,
in a world where there is so much work to be done.
If I am sitting quietly in meditation, or playing music,
shouldn't I be out in the world easing suffering?
If I'm reading a book, shouldn't I be doing something more useful for
the world?
Finding peace is a struggle.
Why?
Because of another word; shame.
How can I be at peace when climate change is upon us?
How can I be at peace when there is so much inequality in the world?
Shame blocks peace.

In my case, the issue which rendered peace unavailable was alcohol;
and the sorrow and sadness accompanying it.

The road back began a long time ago,
but addiction of any sort is a resilient foe.
The shame, and the blues that come with addiction,
linger and find new ways to permeate the mind.
With all this potential for chaos, depression etc. how do I ever find peace?
The toughest mountain for me to climb, is in the fact that during my life,
I have caused hurt to others.
This can grab my mind and hold me in a vice-like grip.
It can own me for a day, or a week, and guarantee me no peace.
Shame.
This is, for me, why peace is elusive.

And yet, peace is not unattainable.
I find peace sometimes; most days in fact.

As is often the case, my path to peace is ultimately quite simple.
And it lies in another word.
That word is surrender.
A much-maligned word.
It is associated with weakness.
It takes courage, humility, and honesty to actually surrender in life.
I had to sink quite low, to get to the point of surrender.
But I did get there.
And surrender is now a daily practise in my life.

If I acknowledge the truth in my life, I find peace.
If I surrender to the mystery of life, I find peace.
If I accept the things I cannot change, I find peace.

If I ask forgiveness for hurt I have caused, I find peace.
If I forgive, I find peace.

The path to peace for me lies in surrender.
Unconditional surrender.
I craved control, and had none.

Now I have no control over any outcome, and somehow, peace is possible.
I stop fighting myself, and the world.
At the beginning of every day, I ask that I be kind.
At the end of every day, if I can identify kindness in that day, there is peace.

I am not a religious man, but every day, I ask the god of my non-understanding, to 'make me a channel of your peace'.
And then, I surrender.

For me, peace is not passive.
It involves action.
Acceptance of life on life's terms.
Gratitude for life itself.
Kindness.
And surrender.
Surrender.

Peace be with you.

. . . .
Luka Bloom is a folk singer-songwriter.

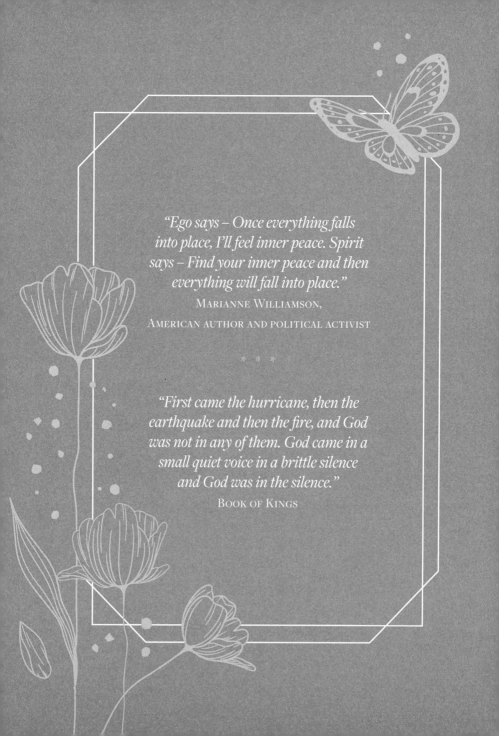

"*Ego says – Once everything falls into place, I'll feel inner peace. Spirit says – Find your inner peace and then everything will fall into place.*"

MARIANNE WILLIAMSON,
AMERICAN AUTHOR AND POLITICAL ACTIVIST

* * *

"*First came the hurricane, then the earthquake and then the fire, and God was not in any of them. God came in a small quiet voice in a brittle silence and God was in the silence.*"

BOOK OF KINGS

A VERY ORDINARY PEACE

Kate Adie

I had a happy, loving childhood – but my parents had been through a war, waiting for the sound of bombers overhead, never knowing when someone might not come home. Afterwards for them, peace was normality. Not just the absence of warfare, but the gentle beat of everyday life, where they could make decisions and plan for the future.

After several happy years as a Jill-of-all-Trades in local radio – farming producer (I know a lot about goats) – terrible DJ, mini-documentary maker, weather forecaster (I occasionally just looked at the sky and guessed), I rather unexpectedly became a journalist. Inevitably, the ills of the world figured largely, especially in international reporting: conflict, disasters, poverty and distress. And the saving grace in that kind of journalism is the hope that people who watch or hear the news reports become more aware of the world – and its needs. And perhaps they might act.

As a reporter, an onlooker, you become aware of how those living in hellish conditions stay human – and humane. The hungry share food. Youngsters kick a ball about in the rubble-strewn street. Strangers offer help, somewhere to stay. A musician plays passionately, even though there is gunfire in the neighbourhood. It is people hanging on to what is normal – and it brings a little peace to them.

Kindness, compassion, friendship – all bring some inner peace.

To open a door – without fear. To walk up the street and see children playing, cats snoozing on windowsills. To hear bad news – and know you can turn to someone who will listen. To hear a kind word – unexpectedly.

Peace, for me, is the sense that we're not alone, that ordinary life with gentle ups and downs is possible.

Kathryn Adie CBE, DL is an English journalist. She was Chief News Correspondent for BBC News between 1989 and 2003, and is considered to be among the most reliable reporters, as well as one of the first British women sending despatches from danger zones around the world. Kate is also the long serving presenter of From Our Own Correspondent *on BBC Radio 4.*

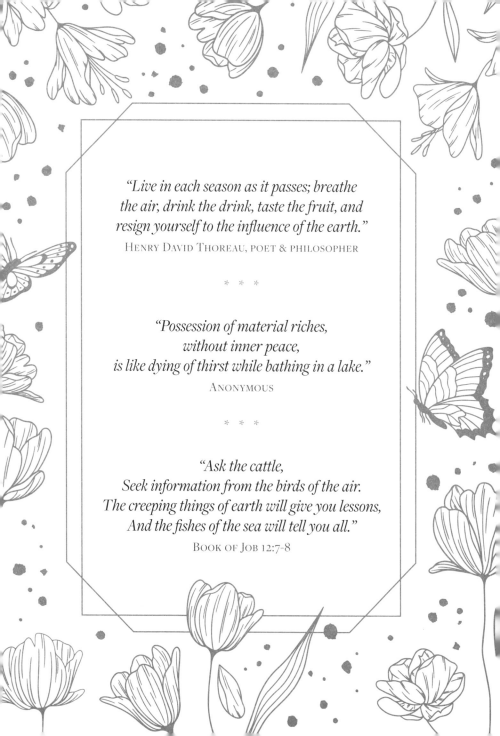

"Live in each season as it passes; breathe the air, drink the drink, taste the fruit, and resign yourself to the influence of the earth."

HENRY DAVID THOREAU, POET & PHILOSOPHER

*   *   *

"Possession of material riches, without inner peace, is like dying of thirst while bathing in a lake."

ANONYMOUS

*   *   *

"Ask the cattle, Seek information from the birds of the air. The creeping things of earth will give you lessons, And the fishes of the sea will tell you all."

BOOK OF JOB 12:7-8

PURE PRESENCE

. . . .

John Quinn

O ur lives comprise a myriad of moments. Moments of joy and sorrow. Moments of pain and delight. Moments of deepest dark and brilliant light. In *The Prelude*, William Wordsworth reminds us that there are moments that retain:

'A renovating virtue when.....our minds
Are nourished and invisibly repaired.'

There are moments of peace, little islands where we find haven from the maelstrom of life. They are often fleeting and can catch us unaware. We need to catch them and savour them for what they are – the leaven that can transform our daily living. A few years ago, I recorded such moments in a journal:

A balmy day in early summer. I am relaxing in my back garden with a mug of tea and my thoughts. Above me, a brilliant blue sky is scarred only by the vapour trail of a transatlantic jet. I am seated under a cherry tree, now in riotous bloom. In a corner of the garden my few drills of potatoes are thriving. Beside me parsley and chives flourish in a terracotta tub. My apple tree promises a rich harvest. The lawn is trim and tidy, thanks to my neighbour who mows it for me regularly. But there are weeds about too. Dandelions dancing in the breeze. Welcome, weeds! All God's children have a place in the choir. Save for occasional twittering's in the hedgerow, there is absolute stillness. The distant church bell chimes three times. A sip of tea. Contentment. So many blessings.....

Moments like those are pure presence. An unearthed gift that truly renovates the mind. They furnish me with an ease that will stay the coming of its enemy, dis-ease. I love the Irish phrase that connotes this feeling – Bhí mé ar mo sháimhín só, I was at my ease. I love it so much that I named my house 'Sáimhín Só' – much more meaningful than 'Fairholme' or 'Bellevue'!

It is interesting that the risen Saviour's first words to his apostles, huddled in the Upper Room in post-Calvary fear and anxiety were 'Peace be with you'. What a blessed greeting to assuage their doubts and calm their fears! Peace. There is such calm in the word itself.

And what if we dreamed of a peace that is not fleeting but forever? Pure presence that would last beyond time? What if it were not a dream but a truth, promised by the Way, the Truth and the Life, who said 'eye hath not see, nor heard nor hath it entered into the heart of man what things God hath prepared for those who love Him'. Pure Presence for all Eternity. Eternal Peace. Ours to realise!

· ·

John Quinn is an author, broadcaster and radio producer.

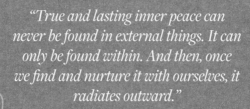

"True and lasting inner peace can never be found in external things. It can only be found within. And then, once we find and nurture it with ourselves, it radiates outward."

Buddha

* * *

"Do stop being anxious and watchful, do not be afraid, for I am your God, I give you strength, I bring you help, I uphold you with my victorious right hand, for I am your God, I am holding you by the right hand and I will tell you do not be afraid, I will help you."

Isaiah 41:10

THE TWO JOANNES

· ·

Joanne O'Riordan

Finding peace throughout my crazy life can be challenging and tricky. Being a writer and a public figure, the primary source of validation for us comes from outside, from editors continually giving you feedback about your content, readers telling you whether or not they like what you're doing, producers giving critique and feedback on everything, and really the outside world just telling you whether they like you or not. Things can get incredibly restless. Suddenly, you find yourself and your inner peace is reliant on all those things.

Instead, I learned that I had two 'selves': the first Joanne is a public persona who is, in a way, incredibly battle-hardened and always goes into the outside world. That Joanne everybody loves. Then there's the internal Joanne, which every day regulates the outside noise, the thirst for social media and approval. The internal Joanne needs to be in harmony with the public Joanne. Otherwise, you find things can get tricky, and it's hard to keep that smile on when your internal self is at war.

So, now, every morning (I won't lie, I do get lazy), I do my best to practice my yoga and really focus on living in the present and essentially work out the internal Joanne. So for 20 minutes, I hop on my yoga mat, do my stretches and my breathing, and really just focus on checking in with the internal Joanne.

Some things are outside your control, what people think of you, outside validation and really a lot of things. Through yoga and mindfulness, I've just learned to not attach my happiness, my identity and my validity to that outside noise. It took time, and boy, am I still learning. But we are all just students in life anyway, taking it day by day, week by week, etc.

Now, with my yoga, meditation and my current understanding, it takes a literal earthquake to disrupt my inner peace. But, at the end of the day, when you then look at the future, the sun will still rise no matter what. Understanding that, along with the fact that I will have more failures and it doesn't mean my goals aren't any way less achievable, has ensured true inner peace.

. . . .

Joanne O'Riordan studied criminology in UCC and is only one of seven people in the world living with a rare physical disability known as Total Amelia. Joanne is an activist for people with disabilities, a motivational speaker and a sports columnist with The Irish Times.

"If you understand this you will know peace. Some things are within the power of your control and some things are not."

Epictetus, Greek Stoic philosopher

* * *

"We must pull ourselves back to the peace within What comes to us from the external has already been said, that which is vital, that which is unique is already within us."

Jon Fosse, Norwegian author & dramatist

* * *

"Do not let your hearts be troubled. Trust in God, trust also in me."

John 14

WORDS ON PEACE

. . . .

President Michael D. Higgins

What I recall as what might be the better moments of peace at a personal level are perhaps those when I was able to be in the company of friends, where it wasn't necessary to explain what friendship was, but merely to enjoy it. I find it difficult to achieve peace in a limited personal sense, particularly if it requires averting one's gaze from where the absence of peace is wreaking havoc in the lives of others. True peace must always be, it seems to me, a troubled peace. I don't think it is morally acceptable to regard a personal peace that distances you from the life and circumstances of others as in any sense sufficient. Yet, when one has put oneself into the agony of others, from such a sharing there is an experience of the greatest peace.

I discern this in *Fratelli Tutti*, Pope Francis' most recent encyclical letter. Indeed, authentic writing out of sense experiences, and informed scholarship, are an inspiration to me and provide a source of succour. The Pope's latest treatise represents a clarion call to discern the depths of our politics and the destructive populism that has engulfed so much of the world in what is undoubtedly a manifestation of a corrosive and far-reaching democratic crisis. It is not merely words on paper. Envisaging, calling to mind, the human source is an uplifting experience.

Pope Francis identifies fraternity and social friendship as the ways to build a better, more just and peaceful world, with the contribution of all – citizens and institutions – and an emphasis on meaningful, inclusive dialogue taken into account. The encyclical also voices an emphatic confirmation of a 'no' to war and to globalised indifference, all of which may assist in the building of a more peaceful, inclusive world.

Pope Francis' observation that peace is connected to truth and justice is a profound one. We in Ireland should also reflect, as we now find ourselves mid-way through the decade of our Centenary Commemorations, on how forgiveness is so often an important prerequisite for peace.

Let us then together cultivate ethical memory as an instrument for the living and as a foundation for the future in order to realise a collective memory at peace, reconciled; an ethical remembering to replace our past entrenchments that represents a foundation of a shared future at peace.

* *

Michael D. Higgins is the current President of Ireland.

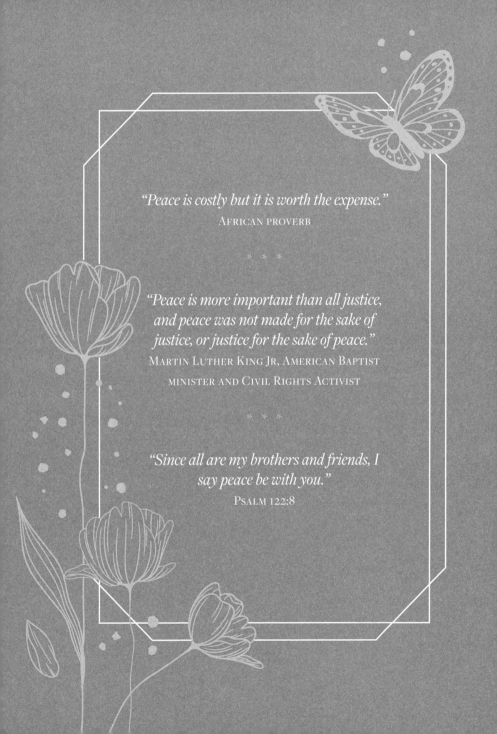

"Peace is costly but it is worth the expense."

AFRICAN PROVERB

* * *

*"Peace is more important than all justice,
and peace was not made for the sake of
justice, or justice for the sake of peace."*

MARTIN LUTHER KING JR, AMERICAN BAPTIST
MINISTER AND CIVIL RIGHTS ACTIVIST

* * *

*"Since all are my brothers and friends, I
say peace be with you."*

PSALM 122:8

PEACE IN MY EVERYDAY WORK LIFE

Nuska Yonkova

My life is quiet but seldom peaceful. The Covid-19 pandemic brought a new silence to my home, along with isolation from people and solitude, yet it took the peace away to some extent. I am constantly trying to remember and reinvent the sources of peacefulness that I used to have.

My work is a series of glimpses in the dark. I need brightness and colours to offset this. What makes me feel peaceful now, more than anything else, is wildflower gardening. This was a new amazing experience that required a bit of labour and very little prior knowledge. The wildflowers in my garden are glorious; a colourful delight, a magnet for the eye. No time seems to be wasted when I am looking at them, at their fragile perfection – shapes, colours, their constantly changing reaction to the weather elements – the sun, the rain, the clouds, the strong wind, the sea breeze.

My flowers love and embrace changes. I admire their ability to adapt, to survive and to come up more peaceful and prettier the morning after a storm had tried to ravish them. Their wee strength is something I discovered for myself. It reminds me of the strength I've seen in women survivors of trafficking and violence – standing strong and wise among us, having overcome unimaginable dark times and ordeals. Aren't these women our wildflowers, our examples of gentle strength and resilience?

This was pretty much what carried me through the loneliness of lockdown. I would bring a chair out and try to work sitting opposite the wildflower patches. I would often be distracted though, as I'd look for my favourites from the day before but instead discover a newer even prettier flower. I would study it, smell it, touch it and take a picture of it. (My mobile phone memory is bursting with flower photos.) Then I would send flower images to people whom I love. Then they would tell me they like them. Then life would be peaceful again.

* *

Dr Nusha Yonkova is a Gender & Anti-trafficking expert at the Immigrant Council of Ireland. Originally from Bulgaria, she is a qualified engineer and holds a Master of Arts Degree in Intercultural Studies from Dublin City University. She became a Doctor of Philosophy at University College Dublin in 2019 with her work 'A Study of Gender Specific Approaches to Assistance of Trafficked, Sexually Exploited Women in Ireland, Bulgaria, Croatia and the UK'.

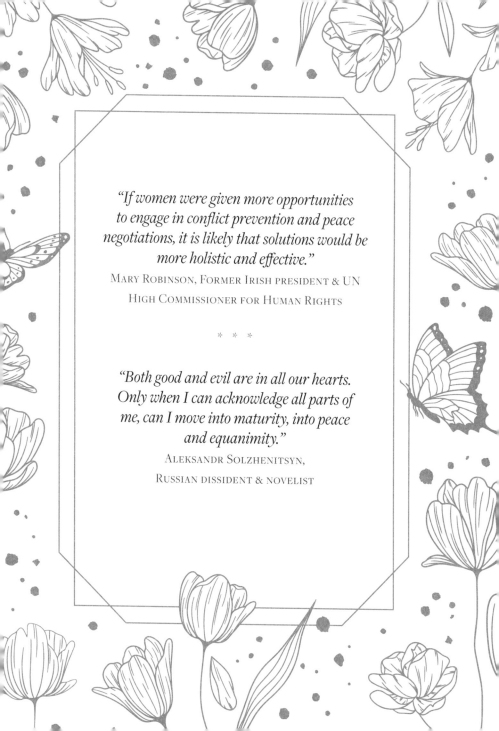

"If women were given more opportunities to engage in conflict prevention and peace negotiations, it is likely that solutions would be more holistic and effective."

MARY ROBINSON, FORMER IRISH PRESIDENT & UN
HIGH COMMISSIONER FOR HUMAN RIGHTS

* * *

"Both good and evil are in all our hearts. Only when I can acknowledge all parts of me, can I move into maturity, into peace and equanimity."

ALEKSANDR SOLZHENITSYN,
RUSSIAN DISSIDENT & NOVELIST

YOU FIND PEACE IN THE JOY

OF OTHERS

· · · · · · · · · · · · · ·

Archbishop Emeritus Diarmuid Martin

I had become used to hearing people ask me, 'Where do you get all your energy from?' When I look back over my diary, I am amazed at the amount of work that passes my way. I am happy being busy. I push myself and get satisfaction from what I do.

Perhaps it was the lockdown. Perhaps it was getting older. Perhaps it was already thinking of what retirement would be like. I began to reflect on how someone like me, who by nature is hyperactive, can really attain inner peace. I came to realise that hyperactivity can get things done, but what people really look to a priest for is finding inner peace.

What are the things that bring me satisfaction? They are all moments when I am able to share the inner satisfactions of others. Alongside hearing horrific stories from victims of abuse, there were moments when survivors could share their joy at how their children had done well despite the hardships they had experienced.

There were moments when you could touch the pride of grandparents as they saw a young grandchild growing to a loving maturity that they themselves could never have dreamed of. There was such joy in what

I call '5 star disadvantaged schools' where all the odds were working against them and then suddenly achievement began to emerge.

I realised that peace came not through looking inwardly at myself. In the midst of a busy life, I could find peace by sharing, even for a short flash, the happiness of others.

Jesus revealed he was God through lifting the burdens that afflicted and troubled so many. His peace came through self-giving, even to the point of giving his life for us out of love.

. . . .

Archbishop Emeritus Diarmuid Martin is the former
Archbishop of Dublin and Primate of Ireland.

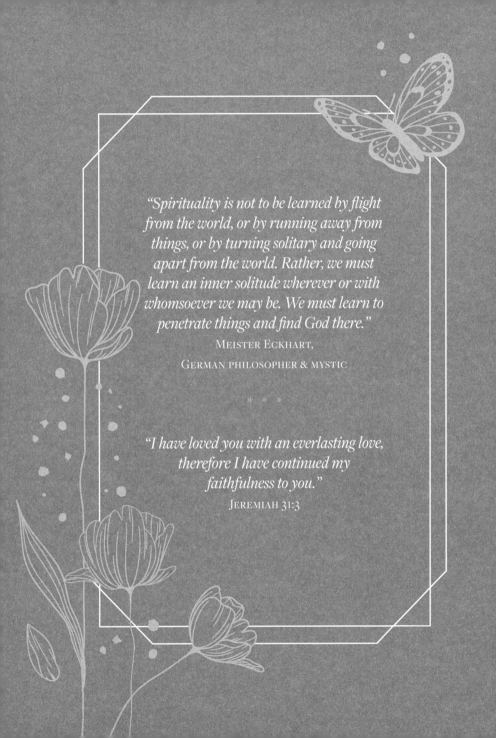

"Spirituality is not to be learned by flight from the world, or by running away from things, or by turning solitary and going apart from the world. Rather, we must learn an inner solitude wherever or with whomsoever we may be. We must learn to penetrate things and find God there."

MEISTER ECKHART,
GERMAN PHILOSOPHER & MYSTIC

* * *

"I have loved you with an everlasting love, therefore I have continued my faithfulness to you."

JEREMIAH 31:3

PEACE WITH YOURSELF

. . . .

Beatrice Epey Ebini

W hy worry about things you cannot control? It sours your mood and makes you less capable. It is vital to ask yourself, is this something I can control? Worrying about situations that are uncontrollable only causes stress and heartaches. As a human being, you have to know which things are within your control. Anything beyond that can distract you and add stress to your life.

There are times in life that we feel depressed and lonely, and sometimes think that people are against us. A situation like this is very unfortunate, and you feel like you are in a race with the universe. Competing with the universe is the most idiotic thing any human being can do. Each time I feel stress and anxiety, I say to myself 'Beatrice, relax, this is just a phase and it will pass.' It is sometimes good to be stressed about life in general, but that only makes us human.

I find peace in my own company and by engaging myself with positive people. Happiness is contagious, by which I mean by staying around positive people you can decrease your stress level. I also find peace by taking control of my life and concentrating more on myself. I have learned the principle of enjoying where I am at the moment, while God is in the process of changing my situation for the better.

I always feel content with myself because I acknowledge that I am not in competition with myself. I accept each day as it comes; this enables me to enjoy and to progress in life. I always try not to focus too much on my weakness, so as not to distract me from progressing. My destiny and time are very important for not letting stress overwhelm me. Assisting others is such a pleasure to me, as I feel good and fulfilled.

Beatrice is studying nursing at Trinity College Dublin. She is a survivor of and an activist against the trafficking of women and girls in Ireland and throughout Europe.

"*Every moment and every event of every man's life plants something in his soul, for just as the wind carries thousands of winged seeds so each moment brings with it germs of spiritual vitality that come to rest imperceptibly in the minds and wills of men. Most of these unnumbered seeds perish and are lost, because men are not prepared to receive them: for such seeds as these cannot spring up anywhere except in the good soil of freedom, spontaneity, and love.*"

THOMAS MERTON. AMERICAN TRAPPIST MONK,
POET AND MYSTIC.

WAR AND PEACE

· ·

Brendan O'Connor

For as long as I could remember I had been at war. At war with myself and with the world. You can even convince yourself it is the noble path. That there is some form of virtue and authenticity in making everything harder, in making life harder. If I didn't put myself through hell to do something, I hadn't done it properly. Pain and conflict were the only worthwhile process or path to anything.

And then, at some point you grow up and you get tired of fighting with yourself, and you realise that seeking some simplicity and some peace is not a cop out.

I run now. I always felt so sorry for those poor people I saw running, looking miserable. But now I run, not even for the physical bit, but more to blow air through my overheated brain. I can sometimes almost see the trail of psychic junk I shed behind me as I run along. I run with fast electronic music sometimes and almost feel like a machine, becoming one with the music, a rhythmic machine. And when I'm finished, for ten minutes, I am the sanest man in the world, unburdened by thoughts.

I can't swim in the pool right now, but I swim in the sea and imagine I am immersing into God or the universal or the primordial soup or whatever. Sometimes in the sea you get precious moments where you feel entirely in flow, briefly at one with the universe, melting into everythingness.

I meditate too. I haven't got it right yet, and I maybe never will, but there are moments of flow and peace there too.

Peace isn't always found in the higher things. Sometimes it's a rasher sandwich and a cup of tea, a game of cards with the kids after dinner, a chat with my mother on the phone. And of course, the greatest shortcut to peace and enlightenment and sanity and connection with others: a good laugh.

Step one of the peace process? Go easy on yourself.

. . . .

Brendan O'Connor is a broadcaster and writer.

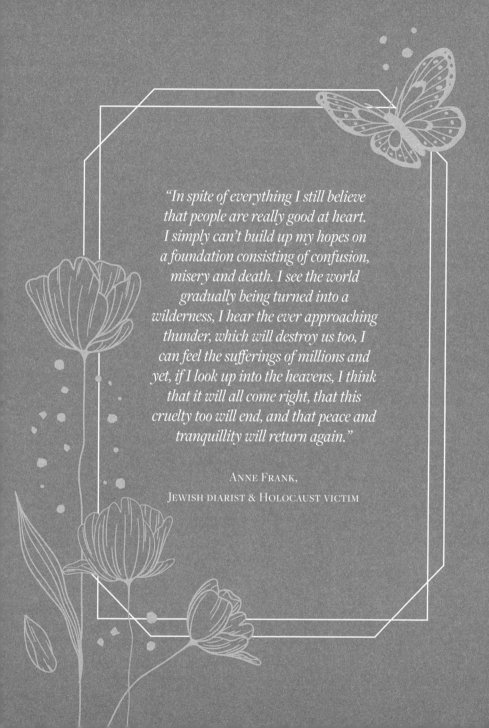

"In spite of everything I still believe
that people are really good at heart.
I simply can't build up my hopes on
a foundation consisting of confusion,
misery and death. I see the world
gradually being turned into a
wilderness, I hear the ever approaching
thunder, which will destroy us too, I
can feel the sufferings of millions and
yet, if I look up into the heavens, I think
that it will all come right, that this
cruelty too will end, and that peace and
tranquillity will return again."

ANNE FRANK,
JEWISH DIARIST & HOLOCAUST VICTIM

MY PEACEFUL MOMENTS

Tomi Reichental

It is my childhood before the Holocaust that reminds me of a peaceful and happy time. The communication was very limited, especially in the rural areas where we lived in a small village called Merasice in Slovakia. I did not know what was happening in the wider world; in fact, I did not know what was happening beyond my village. It was an ideal existence without guilt or care. Still today when I think of my home in Merasice, I still think of it as my paradise.

Pushing time forward 80 years later, life is very different. The world is now in the fast lane. Everybody is in a hurry to earn the extra euro. Living in a city, you cannot find a peaceful place and a moment that is without noise. Cars are buzzing in both directions, in front of your residence or work, while polluting the air. When you pick up a newspaper you feel as though there is a competition for who will print the most distressing news, it is so depressing. There is nothing about good deeds. Where do we find the daily peace we are looking for? It is the little moments that we are not even aware of at the time, which bring peace and happiness to our lives.

I go for a walk with my partner Joyce every day along the banks of the Dodder river, and I look at the beautiful emerald greenery of the Weeping

Willow trees and the river gently flowing by. That is the moment that brings happiness and inner peace to me. Recently I was sitting in my garden; the sky was blue, the sun was shining and the flowers were in full bloom. And I thought to myself, how lucky I am to be able to have this peaceful and happy moment.

. . . .

Tomi Reichental was born in 1935 in Piestany, Slovakia. In 1944 he was deported to Bergen Belsen concentration camp along with his family, where he stayed until he was liberated in 1945. Tomi has lived in Dublin since 1959 and he has tirelessly campaigned, speaking to schools and young people, so that the victims of the Holocaust will not be forgotten.

"Let us not accept violence as the way of peace. Let us instead begin by respecting true freedom: the resulting peace will be able to satisfy the world's expectations, for it will be a peace built on justice, a peace founded on the incomparable dignity of the free human being."

Pope John Paul II

* * *

"Make sure that people do not try to repay evil for evil; always aim at what is best for each other and for everyone."

1 Thessalonians 5:15

PEACE IN OUR DAILY LIVES

An Taoiseach Micheál Martin

I find peace in the ordinary things of life. Meal-times are important, particularly breakfast on busy week days alone with my thoughts. Walking in nature is where I find the greatest peace, observing the changing seasons, listening to the birds singing and surveying the surrounding landscape.

I try to take time out to read, even on a busy day: a newspaper, an article or an extract from a book that has nothing to do with work. Reading calms the mind and creates an alternative narrative and perspective to the world of work.

I find peace in the humour of a well-told story. Laughter is essential to peace of mind. Coming from Cork, the good story-teller is lauded and always enjoys an elevated status amongst the community.

I find peace in the melody of good poetry and during a long working day, a poem or two can do much to lighten the load.

Paradoxically, working hard and diligently brings its own peace of mind, because putting in the hours creatively keeps one's conscience clear and mind at ease, knowing you have left no stone unturned.

Taking time out on a busy day, no matter how short the break, is important. Walking in a nearby park or visiting an empty chapel or simply sitting down and letting the mind wander can help to nurture an inner peace that builds resilience for the storms to come.

Sharing your thoughts with family, friends and work colleagues is key to peace at home and at work. Bottling up your thoughts is negative and damaging. Sharing concerns and anxieties leads to a resolution of perceived problems and difficulties.

This is crucial when working with others who may have different perspectives and who come from different backgrounds. Peace in Northern Ireland was only possible essentially because enough people from different traditions and with different views were open to trusting each other and sharing each other's perspectives, difficulties and fears.

The building up of trust in one's family, community, country and in the world is the essential foundation stone for true peace between peoples.

We all have the potential to find peace in the ordinary everyday things. Striving to share that which unites us all is the best guarantor of PEACE in our daily lives.

. . . .

Micheál Martin is Taoiseach, leader of Fianna Fáil and
TD for Cork South Central.

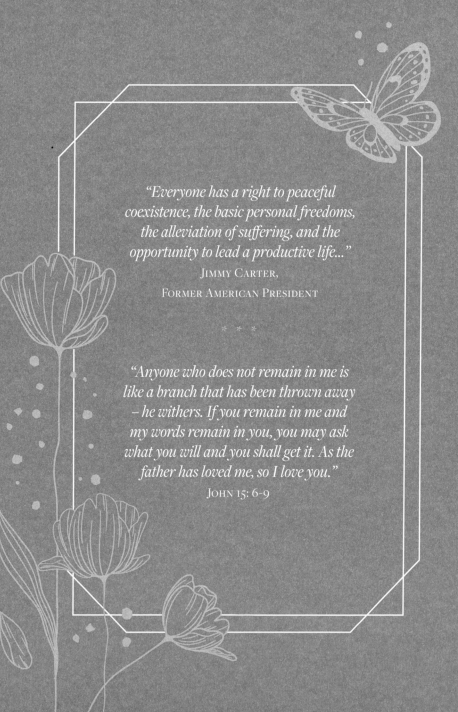

"Everyone has a right to peaceful coexistence, the basic personal freedoms, the alleviation of suffering, and the opportunity to lead a productive life..."

Jimmy Carter,
Former American President

* * *

"Anyone who does not remain in me is like a branch that has been thrown away – he withers. If you remain in me and my words remain in you, you may ask what you will and you shall get it. As the father has loved me, so I love you."

John 15: 6-9

PEACE CLOSE BY

. . . .

Piccola Kelly

I live in a rural area, where there is a wood nearby with a river running down from the hills through it. The river valley stretches inland for about two miles and there is an old ruined folly there with a huge oak, beech, chestnuts, birch, holly and an alder tree at either side of the river. It is sheltered, in all weather, and one can witness each season as it passes.

I feel very much at peace in this marvellous place. The quieter one is, the more of the wild natural world one can see – deer, a red squirrel occasionally, a heron fishing, a kingfisher flying by. One can sit on a mossy bank, or walk along one of the paths on either side, and cross over on the stones when the river is low. One can sit and listen to the sounds of the river and think one's thoughts for a while, admire the trees, the ferns, etc. Each day it feels different.

I go alone or accompanied, and almost always there are two or three people walking their dogs or families out for a stroll. Sometimes there are parties at the old folly and I hear the sound of happy noisy children, probably climbing dangerously, so I escape as quickly as possible. Sometimes there are teenagers having their parties in the evenings, but luckily their party season is brief and weather dependent! The dog walkers and nature enthusiasts are the men for all seasons.

For as long as I'm here, I'll be grateful that I have this oasis of peace to enjoy, just down the road.

· ·

Piccola Kelly is a Dubliner who retired and moved with family to rural Ireland 20 years ago.

"*Meditation is not a way of making your mind quiet. It is a way of entering into the quiet that is already there – buried under the 50,000 thoughts the average person thinks every day.*"

DEEPAK CHOPRA,
ALTERNATIVE-MEDICINE ADVOCATE

* * *

"*I have told you these things, so that in me you may have peace. In this world you will have trouble. But take heart! I have overcome the world.*"

JOHN 16:33

PEACE IN MEANINGFUL ACTION

Brian Cody

I have been asked to write a short piece about how or where I find peace in my life. As I try to get my thoughts together, my mind tends to drift and I find myself wondering about the meaning of peace in our daily lives.

I can't help but imagine what peace means to people who live in countries ravaged by war and famine. Countries where people are exposed to horrors, like watching their families and friends being murdered on a daily basis. Parents hopelessly looking at their children wasting away from starvation not knowing how or where they can get food for their loved ones.

I wonder how possible it is for those trapped in such horrible situations to find peace in their daily lives!

Closer to home we are all well aware of the thousands of homeless people and families in our country. So many others in unfortunate situations struggling to make ends meet.

I think about the anxiety and stress being suffered by so many and then start to consider my own situation.

How privileged am I and many more like me? I don't have to face the situations that confront the people I spoke about above. Does that mean

I am immune from the necessity for peace in my daily life? Of course not, but the solutions are more easily accessed.

Time with my family. A walk in the countryside. A quiet time in meditation or prayer. Sport – winning a few matches. All very ordinary actions but perhaps where peace can really be found in my daily life is when I use my time to benefit others in some meaningful or charitable way.

. . . .

Brian Cody is the manager of the Kilkenny senior hurling team and a former player. He is the longest-serving inter-county manager in the GAA and has won an incredible 11 All-Ireland titles.

"Peace is liberty in tranquillity."

MARCUS TULLIUS CICERO, ROMAN STATESMAN

*   *   *

"Let my doing nothing when I have nothing to do, become untroubled in its depth of peace, like the evening in the seashore when the water is silent."

RABINDRANATH TAGORE, BENGALI WRITER, COMPOSER & PAINTER

*   *   *

"Remain in my love. I have told you these things so that my own joy may be in you, and your joy be complete. This is my commandment; love one another, as I have loved you."

JOHN 15: 10-12

PEACE OF MINE

. . . .

John Robinson

H aving spent the spring and summer of my life working in stressful employment, I decided it was time to change course as I approached the autumn of my years. Some 10 years ago, I entered the gates of the Sanctuary in north Dublin. During my first week, my senses picked up the sound of the birds. I've always compared this experience to my first night in New York City, in a hotel room in the winter of 1978/79, unable to sleep, because of the sound of sirens throughout the night. Two cities, separated by a lifetime, offering contrasting sounds.

I knew nothing about mindfulness or meditation. When introduced to it, I wished I had encountered it earlier in life. My working hours allowed me to experience both day and night-time employment. On gardening days, when alone, the robin would join me. On summer evenings, the blackbird serenaded me.

It soon became apparent that this oasis in the city was indeed a sanctuary to many, including the birds. I discovered that those who visited had either found peace, or were seeking this apparently elusive place. I was aware of the calm and beauty of the place and my life's experience taught me how to 'meet and greet' clients and guests, and to offer assurance and a warm welcome. I am conscious of how nervous everyone is when visiting new places, so kind words of welcome along with a smile reassure them. Sharing an invitation to a place of beauty and calm, where everything and everyone embraces you, is unconditional.

My peace comes from caring and showing understanding for others. Appreciating your own qualities, and using them to put others at ease, is rewarding. Observing the astonishing transformation in people that participate in courses provides an inner peace that is priceless. An open, non-judgemental approach allows peace to enter. Like a smile, it can be contagious.

* *

John Robinson joined the Sanctuary team in 2010, having spent most of his working life in the frantic business world.

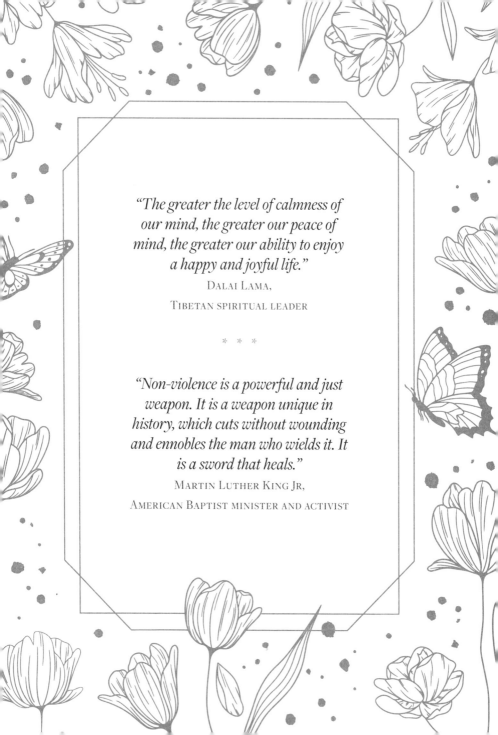

> *"The greater the level of calmness of our mind, the greater our peace of mind, the greater our ability to enjoy a happy and joyful life."*
>
> DALAI LAMA,
> TIBETAN SPIRITUAL LEADER

* * *

> *"Non-violence is a powerful and just weapon. It is a weapon unique in history, which cuts without wounding and ennobles the man who wields it. It is a sword that heals."*
>
> MARTIN LUTHER KING JR,
> AMERICAN BAPTIST MINISTER AND ACTIVIST

POTTERING

· · · · · · · · · · · · · ·

Vera Klute

For me being at peace is a state of complete immersion in an activity or a situation. It is about being completely in the present and accepting it for what it is – not wanting to do anything else; not wanting to be anywhere else; not thinking about anything else.

Some situations lend themselves to this type of carelessness more than others: spreadsheets give me an instant sense of serenity, as does gardening or any other activity that involves a visceral struggle with mud, clay or paint.

Intense concentration and complete carelessness are very close together for me.

Unfortunately as a responsible adult it is not feasible to maintain peace of mind for an extended period of time – it might even be reckless. Being a grown up seems to be all about multitasking, which I believe to be the complete opposite of being at peace. There are so many things that I am supposed to bear in mind at all times, it is a luxury to do only one thing at the one time.

If the Covid-19 lockdowns taught me anything, then it is that most of the points on the mental check-list that I constantly run through don't really matter. It's been a revelation to see how much of the stuff that we get wound up about doesn't matter anymore when it comes to the crunch. The difficult part is deciding what to let go of and what is worth the trouble.

· ·

Vera Klute ARHA is a multi-disciplinary artist. She was born in Germany but is based in Dublin since 2001. She has exhibited widely in Ireland and abroad and her work is part of both private and public collections. In 2014 she was commissioned by the National Gallery to paint Sr Stan's portrait for inclusion in their portrait collection.

[Sonnet 60]
"Like as the waves make towards the pebbled shore
So do our minutes hasten to their end;
Each changing place with that which goes before
In sequent toil, all forwards do contend."

WILLIAM SHAKESPEARE, ENGLISH PLAYWRIGHT

"I will both lie down and sleep in peace;
for you alone, O LORD, make me lie
down in safety."

PSALM 4:8

* * *

"Great peace have those who love your law;
nothing can make them stumble."

PSALM 119:165

STEPPING OUT

· · · · · · · · · · · · · · · ·

Liam ó Maonlaí

Every time I cross the threshold of where I eat and sleep, out into the air and the sky, I feel something. My body feels it. It is as if the stars and the sky connect with what is in me. In autumn, the smell of fallen leaves deepens the experience of breathing for me. I put one foot ahead of the other, as did my people and their people before them. I cease the following of any train of thought but rather allow the thought be and fade. The light of the morning sun feels vivid and nourishing to my being, and I feel buoyed by the light. I walk at an easy pace. Slow and even. This has been a great source of peace for me. To bear witness to the coming of the day as a being of the day. Sometimes at night, in winter, when I walk, I let go of any defence against the cold. I let the cold in, and I become the night. My hands by my side feel the cold and my body no longer feels it as something to run from.

I have paint, ink, charcoal and paper. Often by the fire at home I will play with the colour and the nature of the materials. I let them lead, then I might lead, then they lead again. A dance of creation. I have no goal but to allow a balance between how I feel, what I see, what I feel and how I see. Two days later perhaps, I will take pleasure in gazing at the work as

I might gaze at the sky and the clouds. It is the same with the making of music and although music is my livelihood it is still a source of pleasure and peace for me.

There are many words for God and many stories and ways to adore. I feel blessed to have the air coursing through me. To have the billions of miracles it takes for me to be here, occurring as I write and as you read.

. . . .

Liam ó Maonlaí is a singer and a writer of songs. He is passionate about indigenous culture, his own and those across the earth. He continues to play with Hothouse Flowers and others, and takes deep pleasure and inspiration in doing so.

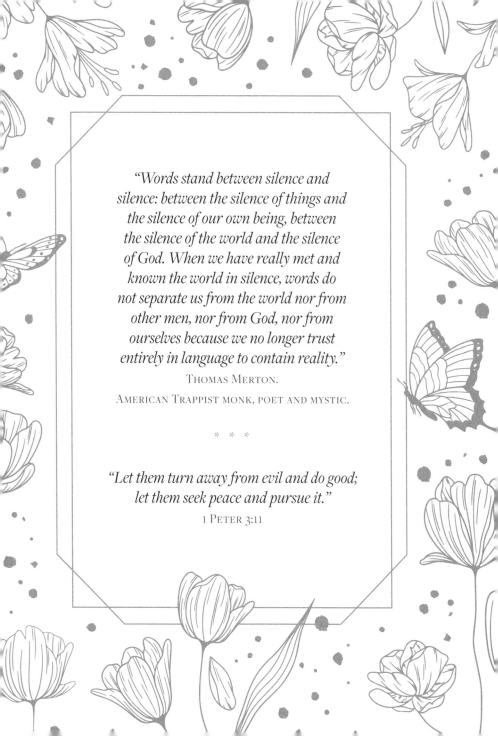

"Words stand between silence and silence: between the silence of things and the silence of our own being, between the silence of the world and the silence of God. When we have really met and known the world in silence, words do not separate us from the world nor from other men, nor from God, nor from ourselves because we no longer trust entirely in language to contain reality."

THOMAS MERTON.
AMERICAN TRAPPIST MONK, POET AND MYSTIC.

* * *

"Let them turn away from evil and do good; let them seek peace and pursue it."

1 PETER 3:11

PEACE MEANS RESPECT FOR DIVERSITY

John Hume

All conflict is about difference, whether the difference is race, religion or nationality. ... Difference is of the essence of humanity. Difference is an accident of birth and it should therefore never be the source of hatred or conflict. The answer to difference is to respect it. Therein lies a most fundamental principle of peace – respect for diversity.

Too many lives have already been lost in Ireland in the pursuit of political goals. Bloodshed for political change prevents the only change that truly matters: in the human heart. We must now shape a future of change that will be truly radical and that will offer a focus for real unity of purpose: harnessing new forces of idealism and commitment for the benefit of Ireland and all its people.

Throughout my years in political life, I have seen extraordinary courage and fortitude by individual men and women, innocent victims of violence. Amid shattered lives, a quiet heroism has born silent rebuke to the evil that violence represents, to the carnage and waste of violence, to its ultimate futility.

I have seen a determination for peace become a shared bond that has brought together people of all political persuasions in Northern Ireland and throughout the island of Ireland.

I have seen the friendship of Irish and British people transcend, even in times of misunderstanding and tensions, all narrower political differences. We are two neighbouring islands whose destiny is to live in friendship and amity with each other. We are friends and the achievement of peace will further strengthen that friendship and, together, allow us to build on the countless ties that unite us in so many ways.

The people of Ireland, in both parts of the island, have joined together to passionately support peace. They have endorsed, by overwhelming numbers in the ballot box, the Good Friday Agreement. They have shown an absolute and unyielding determination that the achievement of peace must be set in granite and its possibilities grasped with resolute purpose.

It is now up to political leaders on all sides to move decisively to fulfil the mandate given by the Irish people: to safeguard and cherish peace by establishing agreed structures for peace that will forever remove the underlying causes of violence and division on our island. There is now, in Ireland, a passionate sense of moving to new beginnings.

And so, the challenge now is to grasp and shape history: to show that past grievances and injustices can give way to a new generosity of spirit and action.

I want to see Ireland – North and South, the wounds of violence healed – play its rightful role in a Europe that will, for all Irish people, be a shared bond of patriotism and new endeavour.

I want to see Ireland as an example to men and women everywhere of what can be achieved by living for ideals, rather than fighting for them, and by viewing each and every person as worthy of respect and honour.

I want to see an Ireland of partnership where we wage war on want and poverty, where we reach out to the marginalised and dispossessed, where we build together a future that can be as great as our dreams allow.

The Irish poet Louis MacNiece wrote words of affirmation and hope that seem to me to sum up the challenges now facing all of us – North and South, Unionist and Nationalist – in Ireland.

'By a high star our course is set. Our end is life. Put out to sea.'

That is the journey on which we in Ireland are now embarked.

* *

John Hume was the former leader of the SDLP Party in Northern Ireland and is regarded by many as the principal architect behind the Good Friday peace agreement. This is an edited extract of his acceptance speech for the Nobel Peace Prize, which he won in 1998 alongside the then-leader of the Ulster Unionist Party, David Trimble. John died in August 2020.

"*Do not worry about anything, but in everything by prayer and supplication with thanksgiving let your requests be made known to God. And the peace of God, which surpasses all understanding, will guard your hearts and your minds in Christ Jesus.*"

PHILIPPIANS 4:6-7

* * *

"*Peace will not come out of a clash of arms but out of justice lived and done by unarmed nations in the face of odds.*"

MAHATMA GANDHI

PEACE AND THE POLITICS OF LOVE

. . . .

Pat Hume

(IN CONVERSATION WITH AINE HUME)

Peace cannot exist alone. It is utterly and completely dependent on the existence of love. For me, peace is defined by those who hold its promise, and live it with love and hope, even when its presence feels very distant. I met many such wonderful people through my life and was sustained by John's own unshakable vision of peace. Peace lives in both public and private spaces. John's work was very public and he was comfortable there, while I have always valued the quiet and private spaces.

Three things have sustained peace for me, even in the most turbulent times I have lived through. The first as I have said, is community, from my own amazing family to the many wonderful human beings I have been privileged to meet. The second is the natural world. I love to walk. I have been blessed to travel a little and I live in Derry, a beautiful city in itself and on the doorstep of Donegal, so beauty is never far away. The third has been quiet moments of prayer. In a busy life, this might have just been a few minutes of quiet in a chapel, or a few moments spoken in my own mind. I have absolutely no doubt that these have sustained my peace, and maybe saved my sanity at times!

When John's parents got married, they had no home. They were given a room by a family who lived in a small terraced house. They had three children in that room, before being given a two-bedroom terrace. They had seven children there and John's uncle and his wife lived in the front room. These experiences helped John develop an unshakeable faith in the generosity of others. His appreciation of human interdependence was fundamental to the way he saw the world. He also understood passionately that difference defines humanity and that embracing diversity is the cornerstone of peace.

We live in uncertain times. If John were alive, he would be applying these three tenets of peaceful change to our current situation. Faith in the generosity of others; trust as a foundation, and above all the embracing of diversity. John's notions of kinship transcended boundaries of family, community and nation. If he were alive today, he would be telling us that our interdependence includes our fragile planet and all the species that live upon it. He would be urging us to develop a planetary kinship. One that is inclusive of all life. This will involve a deep shift in our relationship with the natural world.

Cornell West says that justice is the public face of love. All peace must be underpinned by justice. The approach of non-violence will be central to this. Our experience in Northern Ireland taught me that for those suffering injustice and hardship, violence can offer the seductive illusion of absolute righteousness. Violence blinds both perpetrators and those who fear them, to the messy complexities of human reality. The non-violent path can appear slow and painstaking by comparison. But reality itself is messy and complex and true peace can only be found if it is grounded in reality. It is a lifelong task.

In today's world, violence takes many forms. Wherever there is inequality, injustice and suffering, there is violence. For the millions displaced by conflict and climate change, this is a daily reality. To live peacefully, we need to deepen our understanding of the myriad forms which violence can take. Increasingly, we are learning how exploitation of the natural world is in itself a profoundly violent act, with many consequences.

Our experience of the Covid-19 pandemic taught us that we are part of a single, complex, living system, in which all are profoundly interconnected. Human health and survival are reliant on the wellbeing of our planet and all the living systems which sustain it. Once again, peaceful flourishing depends on our interrelationship with the living world. Watching my grandchildren's generation and their passionate engagement with this gives me great cause for hope.

I have seen many changes in my lifetime. Many of my children and grandchildren's generation reject what they see as the self-protection and power of religious institutions. Having a deep religious faith, and the sustaining rituals and support of being part of a religious community, has carried me through profound challenges. However, I have learned from my own family, friends and community that this is not for everyone and religious doctrine cannot and should not be confused with an ethic of love. Peace is all about relationships and ultimately it is all about love.

· ·

Pat Hume was a former teacher who was married to John Hume for sixty years. She managed his constituency office from his election to the European Parliament in 1979 until his retirement in 2005. She was a member of the Northern Ireland Memorial Fund, the RTÉ Authority and the Spirit of Ireland Awards. She had five children. Pat Hume passed away in Derry following a short illness on 2 September 2021. Her daughter, Aine Hume is married to Kevin Abbott. She is a GP and hospice doctor in Derry. She has four children and two grandchildren.

"There is peace even in the storm."
VINCENT VAN GOGH, DUTCH PAINTER

* * *

*"If we are to have peace on earth, our
loyalties must become ecumenical
rather than sectional. Our loyalties
must transcend our race, our tribe, our
class, and our nation; and this means
we must develop a world perspective."*
MARTIN LUTHER KING JR,
AMERICAN BAPTIST MINISTER AND ACTIVIST

WHERE IS PEACE TO BE FOUND?

Archbishop Michael Jackson

Peace needs to be seen before peace is made or peace is kept. Peace is not a horizon, nor is it a boundary. Peace is the voice of the cosmos itself.

Peace begins with the conversion of the heart and the conviction of the mind: our own and then our personal influence nurtures the peace of everyone we encounter, and in turn everyone they encounter. Peace also defines our relationship with the natural world in all its parts.

Peace therefore needs community of encounter. It is not an individual achievement nor is it a personal treasure. Peace is one of those things you must pass on. You must give it away once you have received it.

The very word: it begs another question. Is peace animate or inanimate? In the religious traditions of the world, peace is more a being than a commodity. In the Christian tradition, phrases from the Scriptures such as The Prince of Peace trip off the tongue and, as we say or hear them, we can see peace as a person offering nurture and healing.

Peace never was, nor can it be, a push over or a soft touch. Peace talks and walks with words like: hope and prophecy; aspiration and expectation. This movement connects peace, time and again, with the secular and the post-secular sphere of influence. If peace is of God, it must be of the world also.

The coronavirus pandemic taught us that hope is indeed in the things not seen. But we have also been taught that the things not seen are present and immediate. Peace is also like this. To be people of peace, we need to weave our strengths and our weaknesses, our limitations and our altruisms into the broad expanse of the cosmos.

Michael Jackson serves as the Church of Ireland archbishop of Dublin and bishop of Glendalough, having previously served as bishop of Clogher.

"My daughter, he said, your faith has restored you to health; go in peace and be free from your suffering."

MARK 5:34

* * *

"I hope you find joy in the great things of life – but also in the little things. A flower, a song, a butterfly on your hand."

ELLEN LEVINE, AUTHOR & LITERARY AGENT

* * *

"The Lord bless you and keep you;
The Lord make his face to shine upon you,
and be gracious to you;
the Lord lift up his countenance upon you,
and give you peace."

NUMBERS 6:24-26

ACCEPTANCE BRINGS PEACE

Corina Duyn

Life is peculiar. Life is never linear. Life can be like a rollercoaster ride which has its gentle moment where one can take a deep breath of relief only to experience those terrifying highs and lows again. Such is life.

For me it is important to find ways to stand still. To get off the rollercoaster and take time to breathe. To observe the experience of what is happening right now. To again find that point in which I am ok with what is. To find acceptance in my heart and mind.

Acceptance is what brings me peace.

For me one of the ways to reach that point of peace is to seek solitude and silence. I have often wondered about the word Stillness: St-illness. Is Stillness the Saint of Illness?

In these moments of silence I observe the world outside my window. I love watching the birds visiting the many feeders in the garden. These feathered friends have taught me about freedom, but also about survival and resilience. No matter what the weather, they have to source food to survive. The birds taught me that although I prefer to fly as freely as a bird, I cannot fly away from the reality of illness.

The lives of my birds also inform and inspire my creative mind. Through words and images I compare our existence and explore the challenges life throws at me. In time I reach a place of peace again, and focus on what is simply necessary or truly beautiful. Having friends and strangers engage with me through my work and words brings me to a place of gratitude. Although I rarely leave my home, the connections I have with people around the world bring positivity in an otherwise challenging situation.

Understanding and accepting my reality brings peace.

• •

Corina Duyn is a 58-year-old Dutch artist and writer who has lived in Ireland for the past 30 years. Twenty two years ago her life changed dramatically due to the onset of the disabling condition Myalgic Encephalomyelitis (ME). Her latest work 'Invisible Octopus' is a poem, a story, an animation of a life triumphant under the weight of illness. Words and images are her lifeline to connect with the world beyond the walls of her home. www.corinaduyn.com

"Peace can only last where human rights are respected, where the people are fed, and where individuals and nations are free."

DALAI LAMA, TIBETAN SPIRITUAL LEADER

* * *

"But the Lord stood by me and gave me strength."

2 TIMOTHY 4:17

* * *

"Keep on doing the things that you have learned and received and heard and seen in me, and the God of peace will be with you."

PHILIPPIANS 4:9

MY COVID STATE OF MIND

P. J. Maher

My mind was racing; it was hard to think positive.
It was like a cup overflowing with water,
It was starting to affect my daily life,
How I felt, how I thought.
Covid-19 was taking control over me and wouldn't let go.
Like a rope pulling at me, tighter, tighter, I couldn't breathe,
I gasped for fresh air, I longed for freedom.

I would try anything to try to escape from Covid-19,
Read, listen to music, watch movies.
Anything to keep my mind from thinking about this.
I kept saying over and over in my mind:
'I won't let it affect me,
I will be strong,
I can do it.'
Over and over in my mind, I would say this; like a mantra,
Until I had banished all negativity.
The negative vibes I was getting from the media wasn't helping.

I was getting more and more depressed,
There seemed to be no light at the end of the tunnel,
Only darkness.

If I gave in to Covid-19, I felt I wasn't me.
I was a creation of Covid-19, a slave to it, that was if I gave in.
But I wouldn't let it beat me, I was a survivor.
Life during Covid-19 isn't easy.
But; it is only a state of mind.
If you believe you can get through it, you will.

P.J. Maher has been a customer of Focus Ireland for about three or four years. He recently moved successfully into accommodation. 'I like singing, reading, watching movies and writing. I'm looking forward to having more time to write now I've settled in my new home.'

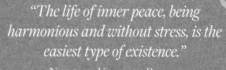

"The life of inner peace, being harmonious and without stress, is the easiest type of existence."

NORMAN VINCENT PEALE,
AMERICAN MINISTER & AUTHOR

* * *

"Better to be poor and walk in integrity than to be crooked in one's ways even though rich."

PROVERBS 28:6

* * *

"And let the peace of Christ rule in your hearts, to which indeed you were called in the one body. And be thankful."

COLOSSIANS 3:15

COMING HOME

· · · · · · · · · · · · · · · · · ·

Tricia McDonnell

M any years ago, I sat by a lake in Scotland and felt such a profound sense of peace that I said to my partner, 'If I knew I had only a few months to live, I would want to spend that time here.'

My choice, given the same situation, would be different now, but since childhood for me being in nature is a balm to my soul. Most days I take time to notice the sky, or the sea, or the moon and the stars, or the trees and the birds.

I think connection brings peace: connection with nature, with family and close friends, and most importantly connecting and re-connecting with myself – coming home to myself.

In work, I witness every day the innate goodness in others. Young people valiantly struggling to overcome childhood trauma. Social care workers choosing to commit to helping them heal. Clients choosing the courageous path of trying to be true to themselves. In all these settings there are moments when a new insight, a new understanding emerges. These connections often bring relief, followed by a sense of peace, which I'm lucky enough to share. The constant reminder of how wonderful people are provides an antidote to the disturbing news we hear all the time.

When I'm at peace, I often experience joy too. This happens for me in the Dances of Universal Peace. Together, we move as one and chant sacred phrases from all traditions. At the end of the dances we finish with chanting: 'May all beings be well, May all beings be happy, Peace, Peace, Peace.' As we dance the sound resonates within and between us. We end with sending that peaceful energy out into the world for the benefit of all.

When the Covid-19 restrictions meant our coming together had to be limited, I would chant this or other sacred phrases most days and occasionally dance on my own! Invariably, a sense of peace washed over me.

Always, it's the simple things that bring me home to myself and to a sense peace.

· ·

Tricia McDonnell is a psychotherapist, trainer and consultant. She has worked predominantly with NGOs and has a particular interest in young people in care. She also leads the Dances of Universal Peace in Malahide, Dublin.

"*Accept what is. Heal and achieve inner peace.*"

Sonia Ricotti, author & personal coach

* * *

"*The greatest misfortune that can come to a human being is to lose his inner peace. No outer force can rob him of it. It is his own thoughts, his own actions that rob him of it.*"

Sri Chinmoy, Indian Spiritual Leader

* * *

"*Those of steadfast mind you keep in peace – in peace because they trust in you.*"

Isaiah 26:3

PEACE IS AN INSIDE JOB

Brian D'Arcy

Mahatma Gandhi was right: 'There is no WAY to peace; there is only peace.' I cannot tell you how to find peace; I share the journey inwards so that we both may find a 'way to peace'.

'Outside God there is nothing but nothing.' This insight came from Meister Eckhart in the 13th century. It's a good 'way' to begin my search for peace.

Patrick Kavanagh has a mystical few lines which I often ponder:

'God cannot catch us
unless we stay in the unconscious room
of our hearts. We must be nothing,
nothing that God may make us something...'

When I accept life as it is rather than what I'd like it to be, inner peace comes. Peace is the fruit of choosing a new way of being; of choosing to be free of the troublesome prejudices of my past.

Peace is not an overcoat to be worn when I feel like it. True peace comes from the inside out; from nothingness to something beautiful... a phrase that reminds me of an incident in Mother Teresa's life.

She visited a well-off parish in the early days of her incredible ministry. As she often did, she told them: 'What you are doing I cannot do and what

I am doing you cannot do. But together we can do something beautiful for the poor and for you.'

Later a parishioner reflected: 'Her secret is that she is free to be nothing. That's why God can use her for anything.'

That's peace.

Peace is more than the absence of war. I accept forgiveness to try to live in the peace-filled present.

There's a difference between peace-keeping and peace-making: the former maintains a kind of peace which often ignores the problem. Peace-making painfully challenges the root causes of the conflict. As a peace-maker I see the world as it is, but also what it can become.

Like William Gladstone: 'We look forward to the time when the Power of Love will replace the Love of Power. Then will our world know the blessings of Peace.'

. . . .

Brian D'Arcy is a member of the Passionist Community. He's a priest for over 50 years. He is a journalist and a broadcaster with the BBC, and a member of BBC Radio 2's Pause for Thought *team for 31 years. He also has a weekly hour-long programme on BBC Radio Ulster.*

"If there's no inner peace, people can't give it to you. Your husband can't give it to you. Your children can't give it to you. You have to give it to you."

LINDA EVANS, AMERICAN ACTRESS

* * *

"All the things that truly matter, beauty, love, creativity, joy and inner peace, arise from beyond the mind."

ECKHART TOLLE, AUTHOR & SPIRITUAL TEACHER

* * *

"May the God of hope fill you with all joy and peace in believing, so that you may abound in hope by the power of the Holy Spirit."

ROMANS 15:13

PEACE — STOLEN MOMENTS IN A BUSY LIFE

. . . .

Claire Byrne

P eace is a valuable commodity in my world!

From the moment the alarm goes off just after 6am, the day is a whirlwind from keeping abreast of the news and work commitments to making sure that my family are ready for their day ahead too. Working on a daily radio show means you're never really 'off' and it's an essential part of the job to keep on top of events as they happen.

Having said that, there are a few snatched moments where peace comes dropping slow. Often, when I'm driving home late from work on a Monday night after my television show, I put on a podcast that I enjoy – one that has no connection to current affairs – and I take a deep breath and listen for pleasure. On other occasions, I will drive in pure silence, which is a rare luxury and affords me a bit of time to let the adrenaline dissipate and to prepare for sleep.

The end of the day is always a time of great peace. There are two essential ingredients – the electric blanket has to be on and properly hot, no half-measures, and a good book on stand-by. I'm often so tired that I will only get through a few pages but it means that I can properly unwind and relax, and it feels like a reward at the end of the day.

Of course, the best place to find peace is in great big hugs with my lovely family – the peace I find at home with them is the peace that really matters.

. . . .

Claire Byrne is a radio and television journalist and broadcaster. She is the presenter of Today with Claire Byrne *on RTÉ Radio One and* Claire Byrne Live *on RTÉ One Television. Originally from County Laois, she is married to Gerry Scollan and they have three children.*

"It isn't enough to talk about peace. One must believe in it. And it isn't enough to believe in it. One must work at it."

ELEANOR ROOSEVELT,
FORMER AMERICAN FIRST LADY

*   *   *

"For the kingdom of God is not food and drink, but righteousness and peace and joy in the Holy Spirit."

ROMANS 14:17

FLYING CROOKED

· ·

Noeline Blackwell

E veryone has their own understanding of peace. As I thought of my contribution to Sr Stan's book, I realised that peace is internal for me, in my head.

My concept of peace is rooted in the belief that the only thing that is certain in this world is uncertainty. Peace is my acceptance of that impermanence. How I link into that inner peace varies. Some might call it haphazard; based on a poem by Robert Graves, I call it 'flying crooked'.

The poem describes a cabbage moth which 'lurches here and here by guess/ and God and hope and hopelessness.' The poet concludes 'Even the acrobatic swift/ has not its flying crooked gift.' Three notions guide my lurching from here to here: gratitude, action and connection to people.

I am grateful for the many gifts that I have been given, to be a woman, to be born and to live in this country, in this age. To have family, friends and colleagues I love, admire and respect. I don't have everything, but I have many, many reasons to be grateful.

I find it soothing to be able to act. Physically, a decent walk will often ground and console me. In my engagement with the world, and my work, I know that there are things I cannot control – but I take consolation from being able to do something.

And while I love my quiet alone time, the Covid-19 pandemic has shown me the deep joy that I get through my connection with other people. Like many, I missed that wider human interaction we took for granted before the pandemic, where the sheer extraordinariness of human beings kept me interested and amused – a great way to be at peace.

Noeline Blackwell is a human rights lawyer and CEO of the Dublin Rape Crisis Centre. She currently chairs the Independent Patient Safety Council and the Child Care Law Reporting Project. She sits on the Department of Foreign Affairs & Trade's Women Peace & Security Oversight Group and its Audit Committee, and is a member of UCD's Governing Authority.

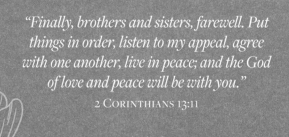

"Finally, brothers and sisters, farewell. Put things in order, listen to my appeal, agree with one another, live in peace; and the God of love and peace will be with you."

2 CORINTHIANS 13:11

* * *

"If it costs your inner peace, it is too expensive."

ANONYMOUS

* * *

"So we do not lose heart. Even though our outer nature is wasting away, our inner self is being renewed day by day."

2 CORINTHIANS 4:16

PEACE FROM QUIET REFLECTION

Leo Varadkar

I try to find peace in moments of quiet reflection and in the company of friends and loved ones. It's something I actively seek out, both for my own well-being and so that I can do my job to the best of my ability. In times of crisis, when we spend most of our time thinking and worrying about others, I also think that we need to find some time to look after ourselves.

I try to schedule quiet times for reflection every day and I try not to spend the precious few spare minutes I have scrolling on my phone or distracted by social media. These peaceful moments help me clear my head. You make better decisions when you give yourself time to make them; when you don't simply react to things and when you are able to plan for the future.

I believe that a healthy body helps promote a healthy mind and a general wellbeing. So I try to get to the gym or out for a run a few times every week. I use the time to listen to music and switch off from the noise all around me. Very often I find that it helps me make sense of everything that is going on and I return to work able to think about old problems in new ways.

At the end of a long day I try to spend a few moments in meditation and quiet reflection. I am grateful for the good things in my life and the people around me. I think of the things I got wrong and I resolve to do better the next day. It's not quite prayer, meditation or mindfulness, but it's something like it.

Leo Varadkar, TD is Tánaiste and Minister for Enterprise, Trade and Employment, and Leader of Fine Gael, Dublin West.

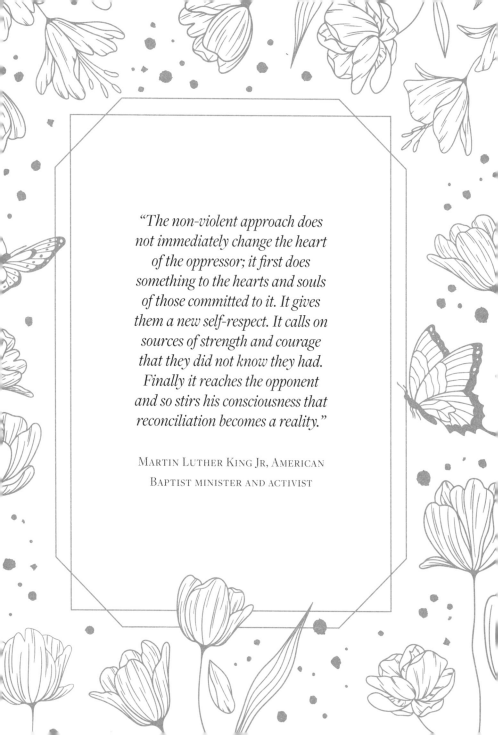

"*The non-violent approach does not immediately change the heart of the oppressor; it first does something to the hearts and souls of those committed to it. It gives them a new self-respect. It calls on sources of strength and courage that they did not know they had. Finally it reaches the opponent and so stirs his consciousness that reconciliation becomes a reality.*"

Martin Luther King Jr, American
Baptist minister and activist

LIFE, IN PIECES

. . . .

Joe Duffy

Why, during the great Covid-19 pandemic, as every sinew of our lives was savagely disconnected, did people turn to solitary pursuits? For me, as well as dabbling in watercolours, there was walking, reading and indoor swimming – the latter disappeared during the lockdown. I know some people have found their tribe swimming in the icy Irish Sea – but I haven't lost my mind, yet!

Then from out of the blue I became obsessed with jigsaws. I always saw jigsaws as arcane endeavours, which usually fetch up in the middle of a cruise ship in Agatha Christie murder mysteries.

The lure is very simple – jigsaws are about making order out of chaos. In a world turned upside down and inside out by the coronavirus rollercoaster, we were able to create an interlocked, linked world, where every single thing has its place, and once joined together – often with great difficulty – completes the picture.

Anyone, even if you cannot read or write, can do a jigsaw. They are an exercise for the brain, which leads to a better mood that comes with achievement, and they are inexpensive. As you become engrossed in the jigsaw, you can relax, listen to music, the radio or the quiet humming of precious, calming, meditative silence.

The brain has to be focused; it's not just your fingers that get a workout doing jigsaws, you become so engrossed you are close to mindfulness! Apparently, jigsaws ignite the left side of our brain through the challenge and the right side by looking for the bigger picture.

Childhood memories are evoked when you open a jigsaw, the avalanche of pieces cascading on to the table is not just a lovely sound – it's a beautiful tactile sensation. There are no limits to the number of people who can 'help' doing a jigsaw. It may take a long time to get it right, but you can't get it wrong. They are not just a break away from our demanding solitary digital world, jigsaws have only one mission in life – to be complete!

Just like humans.

· ·

Joe Duffy is a radio and TV broadcaster, author and columnist.

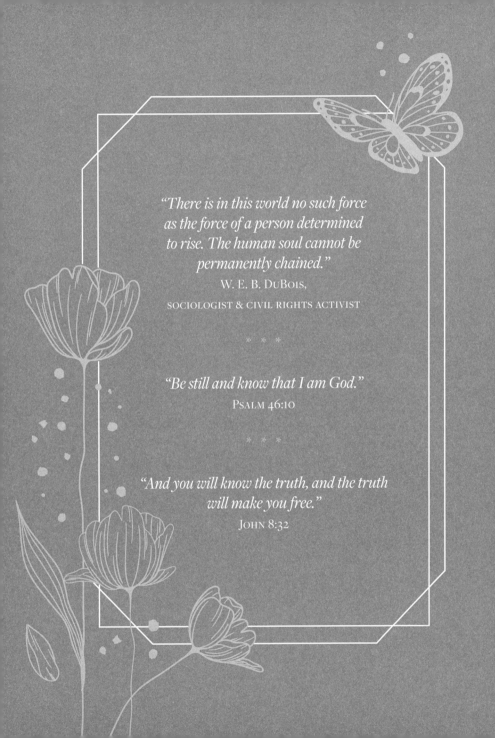

"*There is in this world no such force as the force of a person determined to rise. The human soul cannot be permanently chained.*"

W. E. B. DuBois,
SOCIOLOGIST & CIVIL RIGHTS ACTIVIST

* * *

"*Be still and know that I am God.*"

Psalm 46:10

* * *

"*And you will know the truth, and the truth will make you free.*"

John 8:32

FRATELLI TUTTI

. . . .

Pope Francis

In his encyclical *Fratelli Tutti* Pope Francis calls for peace and fraternity:

118. The world exists for everyone, because all of us were born with the same dignity. Differences of colour, religion, talent, place of birth or residence, and so many others, cannot be used to justify the privileges of some over the rights of all. As a community, we have an obligation to ensure that every person lives with dignity and has sufficient opportunities for his or her integral development.

127. Certainly, all this calls for an alternative way of thinking. Without an attempt to enter into that way of thinking, what I am saying here will sound wildly unrealistic. On the other hand, if we accept the great principle that there are rights born of our inalienable human dignity, we can rise to the challenge of envisaging a new humanity. We can aspire to a world that provides land, housing and work for all. This is the true path of peace, not the senseless and myopic strategy of sowing fear and mistrust in the face of outside threats. For a real and lasting peace will only be possible 'on the basis of a global ethic of solidarity and cooperation in the service of a future shaped by interdependence and shared responsibility in the whole human family'. [108]

225. In many parts of the world, there is a need for paths of peace to heal open wounds. There is also a need for peacemakers, men and

women prepared to work boldly and creatively to initiate processes of healing and renewed encounter.

231. Negotiation often becomes necessary for shaping concrete paths to peace. Yet the processes of change that lead to lasting peace are crafted above all by peoples; each individual can act as an effective leaven by the way he or she lives each day. Great changes are not produced behind desks or in offices. This means that 'everyone has a fundamental role to play in a single great creative project'.

A PRAYER TO THE CREATOR
Lord, Father of our human family,
you created all human beings equal in dignity:
pour forth into our hearts a fraternal spirit
and inspire in us a dream of renewed encounter,
dialogue, justice and peace.
Move us to create healthier societies
and a more dignified world,
a world without hunger, poverty, violence and war.

May our hearts be open
to all the peoples and nations of the earth.
May we recognise the goodness and beauty
that you have sown in each of us,
and thus forge bonds of unity, common projects,
and shared dreams.
Amen

His Holiness, Pope Francis.

"While you are proclaiming peace with your lips, be careful to have it even more fully in your heart."

FRANCIS OF ASSISI

* * *

"The wisdom from above is first pure, then peaceable, gentle, willing to yield, full of mercy and good fruits, without a trace of partiality or hypocrisy."

JAMES 3:17

* * *

"Those who deny freedom to others deserve it not for themselves."

ABRAHAM LINCOLN,
FORMER AMERICAN PRESIDENT

PEACE IS THE WAY

Tony Bates

'Could you write something about peace?' she asked. 'Of course', I replied. Two months later, I still haven't made good on my promise. I sit at my screen, wondering why such a familiar word is proving so hard to pin down.

Peace is proposed as the solution to conflicts that destroy communities all over the world. Inner peace is the recommended panacea for surviving this frantic world and protecting our health. Peace, it would appear, is the golden ticket to a brave new world.

Peace is generally described in terms of the absence of anxiety, sorrow or anger in our personal lives, and the absence of violence, cruelty and injustice in our communities. I wonder how realistic it is to imagine a world where people live without conflict.

I'm more interested in a peace that empowers us to step into the heat of battle rather than escape it. Ballast that allows us to walk through a storm without being over-powered by it.

Such a peace begins with facing reality. We first need to enter into our own hearts and accept what we find there. As long as we are at war with ourselves, we can only sow seeds of division in an already divided world.

Acceptance allows us to face the truth of our own lives. When we engage with life from a place of truth, we engage in an open and authentic way. We align our values and behaviour with what we deem to be most important. We bring humility and peace to whatever crisis we encounter. We believe that what is negative in life need not have the last word. That despite the darkness, all can be well.

There is no way to peace; peace is the way.

· ·

Tony Bates is a Clinical Psychologist and Honorary Professor of Psychology in UCD. He is the Founder of Jigsaw – The National Centre for Youth Mental Health. Author of Coming through Depression: A Mindful way to Recovery, *he now lives on a cliff in North Sligo with four chickens, three cats and a pair of rabbits.*

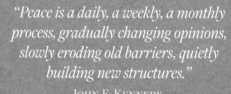

"Peace is a daily, a weekly, a monthly process, gradually changing opinions, slowly eroding old barriers, quietly building new structures."

JOHN F. KENNEDY,
FORMER AMERICAN PRESIDENT

* * *

"I therefore, the prisoner in the Lord, beg you to lead a life worthy of the calling to which you have been called, with all humility and gentleness, with patience, bearing with one another in love, making every effort to maintain the unity of the Spirit in the bond of peace."

EPHESIANS 4:1-3

SIMPLE THINGS BRING GREAT PEACE

Mary Coughlan

I'm actually not very good at writing about such things and as someone who struggled all my life to find peace, I've found that really simple things bring great peace into my heart ... even if it's for a few moments at a time.

I meditate every morning. I find even 15 minutes calms my head down and sets me up for the day...

If things in my life begin to overwhelm me, I take off my shoes and socks, and stand outside on the Earth and take seven long slow breaths. I find myself doing this more and more during these troubled times we're living in... I stand outside under the full moon... or any moon for that matter...

My grandchildren and I frequently look at the stars and wonder. We have spotted the International Space Station a few times and we wondered what it might be like to travel around the Earth...

I walk around the Little Sugar Loaf Mountain and I stop along the way to look for faces in the trees. I find them every day. I take photos of them and send them to my sister and we discuss who they might be.

Most of the time, I sing while I'm walking. I open my mouth and just let it all go!

I remember to be grateful for this gift every day.

I remember to be grateful every day for all the joy and love I have in my life.

. . . .

Mary Coughlan is a singer, songwriter and actress.

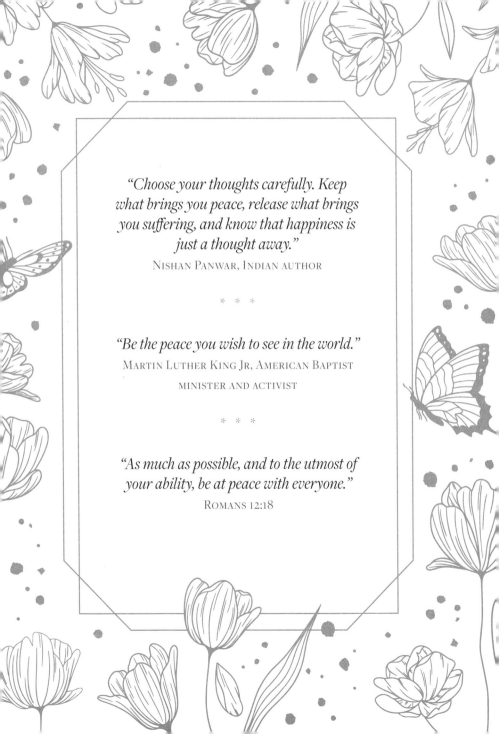

"Choose your thoughts carefully. Keep what brings you peace, release what brings you suffering, and know that happiness is just a thought away."

Nishan Panwar, Indian author

* * *

"Be the peace you wish to see in the world."

Martin Luther King Jr, American Baptist minister and activist

* * *

"As much as possible, and to the utmost of your ability, be at peace with everyone."

Romans 12:18

FINDING PEACE IN THE PICTURE

Bishop Alan McGuckian

I have a picture of the Sacred Heart of Jesus on the wall of my office opposite my desk. Much of the time I forget that he's there and when I do look up at him it's often with a rueful smile. ('How did we get into this fix?') I'm looking at him right now and I want him to tell me how and when I find peace in the everyday because I believe, deep down, that he is my peace.

Peace, as a felt experience, comes and goes. I live with a certain amount of worry; it's the sort of personality I came to have. I'm a bit like the swan gliding along 'effortlessly' on the surface while under the water the legs and feet are going at ten to the dozen. It doesn't take much to spark it off or fan it into a blaze. Very often I find myself wishing it were not so! But, a lot of the time it is so and what are we to do?

When I'm not at peace I have to interrogate the situation. What's going on here? The Jesuits taught me a lot about how to do that in the Daily Examen. Sometimes, I'm not at peace because my life is out of order; I'm clinging to something that is not good for me and I need to let it go. Repentance. Other times I'm dealing with a situation that is genuinely challenging; I have to put up with some distress until it passes. What really bugs me are the times I live with a debilitating cocktail of panic and worry about what might happen. Most of the time I realise it's all in my head.

My peace is something deep down. That ultimate peace I don't give to myself. It has been given to me. Often I just rely on the conviction that it is there even if I don't feel it in the moment. Partly it is simply a conviction that all will be well and it is also a person. The one in the picture on the wall.

. . . .

Bishop Alan McGuckian SJ is a native of North Antrim. After years of service as a Jesuit priest in Clongowes, Dublin and Belfast he was ordained Bishop of Raphoe in 2017. He lives in Letterkenny.

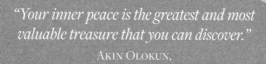

"*Your inner peace is the greatest and most valuable treasure that you can discover.*"

AKIN OLOKUN,

AUTHOR & HEALTH FOOD ADVOCATE

* * *

"*Inner peace is priceless as it sprinkles everything you do with joy.*"

ROZ FRUCHTMAN, AMERICAN DIGITAL ARTIST

* * *

"*Let me hear what God the Lord will speak, for he will speak peace to his people, to his faithful, to those who turn to him in their hearts.*"

PSALM 85:8

THE SEA CURE

· · · · · · · · · · · · · · · · · · ·

Mary Fitzgerald

The sea, the sea, the sea! Whether the Atlantic, the Mediterranean or several others in between, some of the happiest and most eventful chapters of my life have unfolded by oceans and seas. After a career that has taken me to many different corners of the globe, I have come to realise the special connection those of us born on a small island feel with the sea.

In recent years, the Mediterranean has become my home. I lived first in Tripoli, the capital of Libya, and now in Marseille, the second city of France. From my perch in this storied city shaped by millennia of immigration, the Mediterranean that spreads out before me each morning is a reminder of shared histories and the exchange of people, goods and ideas between east and west. It's a sea that soothed when I lived on its southern rim and walked the Tripoli corniche each day as Libya slowly tipped into civil war around me. It continued to be a balm when I moved to Marseille still grieving friends and colleagues killed in Libya and Syria.

A swim at dawn. A stroll or a run along the coastline after a heavy day of work. A beach picnic with friends. A quiet moment alone listening to the waves crashing as the setting sun disappears below the sea line.

The Covid-19 pandemic challenged us all. During months of lockdown – or confinement as the French call it – in Marseille, the Mediterranean was my antidote to the uncertainty that swirled across the world. That sea is my tonic, its horizon a reminder of the need to keep looking forward, its history a reminder that everything – including pandemics – passes. When our new mayor – the first woman to hold the post – was elected last year, she quoted a famous line from novelist Blaise Cendrars: 'Marseille belongs to those who come from the open sea.' It's a line I have long loved because it means my adopted city belongs to everyone.

* *

Mary Fitzgerald is a writer and consultant specialising in the Euro-Mediterranean region, with a particular focus on Libya. From Cork, she began her career as a journalist in post-conflict Northern Ireland. Since then she has won several awards and fellowships for her work. She reported from more than 40 countries as a roving staff foreign correspondent for the Irish Times *and also wrote a column on international affairs for the* Irish Independent.

"*The starry sky is the truest friend
in life, when you've first become
acquainted; it is ever there, it gives
ever peace, ever reminds you that your
restlessness, your doubt, your pains
are passing trivialities.*"

ERLING KAGGE, NORWEGIAN EXPLORER,
AUTHOR, LAWYER AND POLITICIAN

* * *

"*The fruit of the Spirit is love,
joy, peace, patience, kindness,
generosity, faithfulness.*"

GALATIANS 5:22

PHONELESS FOR PEACE

Justin Mc Aleese

I found this question difficult to answer. My first port of call was to ask my husband Fionán how he thought I found peace in my life. He said, 'Are you ever peaceful?' Not a great start. I then asked our Amazon Alexa device. She said, 'Sorry, I'm not sure.' It was becoming clear that I was going to have to answer this question on my own.

On. My. Own. That is my answer! I have always been comfortable in my own company. One of my favourite things to do is to escape the office for lunch on my own, without my phone, a couple of times per week. I have friends and colleagues who could not think of anything worse than sitting on your own in a café. I could not be happier – sitting in my own thoughts, people-watching and taking in what is going on around me.

Our mobile phones have made us accessible 24/7 and bombard us with a lot of noise. For me, disconnecting from that noise for a short time every day is essential to finding peace and calm. Every day I go for a run or a walk and I do it without my phone or earphones. Instead of getting lost in a podcast or being interrupted by a call, I pay attention to what is going on around me. Whether it's tracking the changing colour of the leaves or giving the nod to the dog that is always in the drive or smiling at a parent and child walking to school. There are no memes, no videos, no messages – just the real world going on around me. Try it. Turn the phone off for half an hour and have a coffee or a walk on your own.

. . . .

Justin McAleese is a chartered accountant and council member of the President's Award – Gaisce.

"If we have no peace, it is because we have forgotten that we belong to each other."

MOTHER TERESA, MISSIONARY & SAINT

* * *

"Fasten the belt of truth around your waist, and put on the breastplate of righteousness. As shoes for your feet put on whatever will make you ready to proclaim the gospel of peace."

EPHESIANS 6:13-15

PEACE IN AN OLD FASHIONED WAY

Mary Kennedy

The Covid-19 pandemic made me realise that for me peace and a feeling of wellbeing enter my life through the prism of connection with other people. During the first lockdown I made the occasional phone call to people that I hadn't seen in a while. A cuppa in one hand and the phone in the other, lying on the couch. And just chatting! I was surprised and delighted how lovely it was to make contact out of the blue with an old pal or colleague and just catch up in the old fashioned way of lifting the phone. It was a case of having a conversation, in the moment, with a person and asking them how they were getting on. Some were getting on okay, others were struggling. In all cases though, the phone call was a joy for me and I hope it was pleasant for them too.

The daily phone call to someone that I don't see regularly has become a habit now. I look forward to making contact and engaging in a human and real way with another person – such a different experience from texts, emails and tweets. In all cases, the phone calls provide a moment of nice connection during the day. They lift my spirits and bring me a feeling of peace, calm and warmth. And they are a reminder of the truth in Antoine de Saint-Exupéry's words:

'There is no hope of joy except in human relations.'

Mary Kennedy is a broadcaster and has worked on many RTÉ programmes including Open House, Up for the Match, Christmas Eve Carols, Eurovision Song Contest *and* Nationwide. *She recently presented* Guaranteed Irish *on TG4. She is the author of five books of personal reflections, the latest is* Home Thoughts from the Heart.

"Peace comes from being able to contribute the best that we have, and all that we are, toward creating a world that supports everyone. But it is also securing the space for others to contribute the best that they have and all that they are."

HAFSAT ABIOLA,
NIGERIAN HUMAN RIGHTS ACTIVIST

* * *

"May the Lord give strength to his people!
May the Lord bless his people with peace!"

PSALM 29:11

PEACE IN THE LIVING MOMENT

Theo Dorgan

For me being at peace means living in heightened, unstressed, attention to the self and to what is other; it has to do with conscious awareness of the self and its place in the world in the living moment – engagement without tension, paying attention, being receptive, accepting the given, taking simple joy in being alive and being aware of it.

There is peace in sitting by the fireside, gazing upon someone you love, marvelling at the simple fact of their existence. There is peace in companionable silence, attuned to some other, fully and simply attentive to each other. There is peace to be found in work, in being fully immersed in some satisfying, solitary task or in working quietly in company with others.

By way of illustration, I call to mind a time when four of us were bringing a big boat up to Ireland from the Caribbean. To be at the wheel with the others asleep below, trusting their lives to you; to be driving from dark into dawn, all sails full and pulling, the hull carving straight and true in the heavy seas, the wind freshening and every twitch of the boat's response feeding through to your fingertips — that was a kind of living, active peace; a sense of sureness in the world and in the self.

In the Southern Ocean, in another time, in dangerous waters, there was a peace to be found in the comradeship of the crew, each at his or her own task on deck but working together to a common end — call it the peace of working together in mutual trust. My point is a simple one: being at peace is not a state of withdrawal or subtraction, it comes with being fully committed in and to the living moment.

* *

Theo Dorgan is a poet, a non-fiction prose writer, novelist, editor, documentary screenwriter, essayist, librettist and translator.

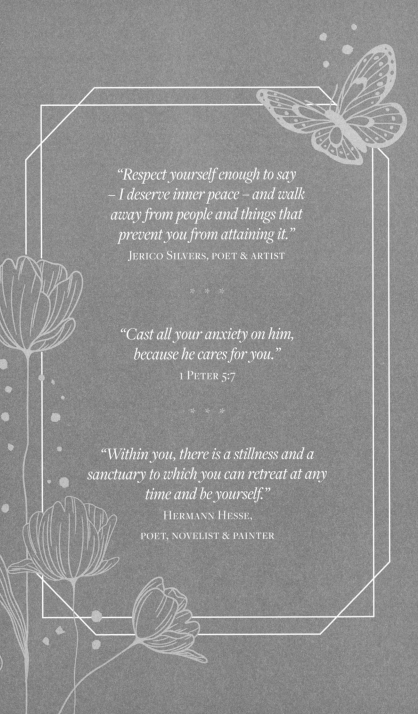

"Respect yourself enough to say – I deserve inner peace – and walk away from people and things that prevent you from attaining it."

JERICO SILVERS, POET & ARTIST

* * *

"Cast all your anxiety on him, because he cares for you."

1 PETER 5:7

* * *

"Within you, there is a stillness and a sanctuary to which you can retreat at any time and be yourself."

HERMANN HESSE,
POET, NOVELIST & PAINTER

THE SEARCH FOR INNER PEACE

Harry Barry

I find inner peace in the unconditional acceptance of myself and others as the wonderfully unique, if innately flawed, human beings that we are. Where I cannot be measured, judged or rated as a person. Where I try to do my best in relation to my actions and behaviours, accepting that sometimes my best efforts will fall short of the ideal, but that too is ok.

I feel inner peace flowing through my veins as I immerse myself in Mother Nature. In the silent beauty of the forest. In the roar of the mighty ocean waves. In the beauty and calm of our lakes and rivers. In the freedom and colour of the birds of the air and the flowers which adorn our gardens and parks. In the majesty of the mountains. In the wondrous constantly changing landscape of my beloved Burren hills. In the majesty of sun-kissed mighty Atlantic waves breaking onto the shorelines of County Clare. In the buffeting winds and haunting beauty of the Flaggy Shore, so beloved of Yeats and Heaney. In the wonder and beauty of the star-filled sky, and the immensity of the universe.

Finally, I find inner peace in my life-long search for meaning. I have found this in the arms of the person I love, in my children and grandchildren, who root me in what truly matters in life. In the wonderful people who have been sent to enrich my life. In service to others, who have allowed me the privilege of walking the often painful journey of life with them. In those who have gone before me, and with whom I hope one day to be re-united. In beautiful music and art. In the spirit. In love.

May peace too find you.

Harry Barry is a GP and author of numerous books addressing mental health.

*"Blessed are the peacemakers, for they will
be called children of God."*

MATTHEW 5:9

*   *   *

*"Inner peace can be seen as the ultimate
benefit of practicing patience."*

ALLAN LOKOS,
AMERICAN AUTHOR & MEDITATION TEACHER

*   *   *

*"May the God of peace himself sanctify you
entirely; and may your spirit and soul and
body be kept sound and blameless at the
coming of our Lord Jesus Christ."*

1 THESSALONIANS 5:23

EVERYDAY PEACE

. . . .

John Dardis, SJ

S ince coming to Rome, one of my favourite places is the terrace of our Jesuit house here. There I find a peace and a serenity far from the bustle of the city. The house itself is a bit like a military barracks, functional rather than aesthetic. But from the terrace on the fifth floor you can see right over the Vatican which, at night, is just lit up so brilliantly. I walk up and down and let the day pass through me. I don't even know if this is prayer, but often I feel that God is gently leading me, calming me, giving me depth and perspective. I get some insight about the work of the day or about myself or about relationships. All of that helps me start the next day on a different footing, kinder towards myself and others.

Another way I find peace is as I am getting up in the morning I listen to morning prayer in Italian on my phone. There is something about the singing, the music of the Italian language, the connection to community that is so precious and so calming.

God reaches out to us in so many ways, throughout each day. He is the God of compassion and love; the God of mercy and forgiveness; the God of peace and healing. I have had to learn to find this God, this real God, to let former images from harsher times melt away and to be in peace. Finding this peace is not always easy for someone with an active personality like my own. I like to get things done, to move things forward. But I treasure these moments. They keep me humble, dependent on someone rather than on what I myself can achieve.

Jesus can change our lives radically, giving us hope, peace and healing where we need it most. If I can say one thing it will be – Don't underestimate God. God is reaching out to you; through friends, family, through nature, through the Church with all its flaws and failings. You need not live your life unhealed or wounded. God can heal you. God can surprise you. God can give you peace.

· ·

John Dardis, SJ is the General Counsellor for Discernment & Apostolic Planning and Director of Communications in the General Curia of the Society of Jesus in Rome.

"*Freedom is dearer than bread or joy.*"
JESSIE E. SAMPTER,
AMERICAN POET & JEWISH EDUCATOR

* * *

"*The well-being and the hopes of the peoples of the world can never be served until peace – as well as freedom, honour and self-respect – is secure.*"
RALPH J. BUNCHE, AMERICAN POLITICAL
SCIENTIST & DIPLOMAT

* * *

"*Peacemakers who sow in peace reap a harvest of righteousness.*"
JAMES 3:18

AWAKENING PEACE

· ·

Sile Wall

R estless mind
Yearning for peace

Imprisoned through conflict
Looking for peace

Distraught with worry
Hoping for peace

Overwhelmed by pain
Seeking peace

Submerged by poverty
Crying for peace

Tormented heart
Searching for peace

At our deepest core, at the core of our creaturehood, we all have the seeds of suffering. If we haven't experienced or acknowledged this part of ourselves, we cannot really desire or know peace. The corollary is also true, somewhere at the core of our being seeds of peace are awaiting life.

The yin and yang of life is a mystery. The desire for peace means choosing peace and in the choosing, over time, making peace with what is. The choosing and the experience, however that might be for each of us, are intertwined.

For me it's the in-between time, those ordinary everyday moments when I'm intentionally in awe at the wonder of nature; engrossed in a particular colour hue; or sitting quietly in meditation/prayer – that the seeds of peace are nourished, creating space that can allow my inner and outer worlds to meet in harmony and in peace.

* *

Síle Wall is a member of the congregation of the Religious Sisters of Charity and assisted Sr Stan in founding and developing the Sanctuary as a meditation centre for social change. Her professional background includes social work, community work and art therapy. She has also contributed essays and poems to a number of publications.

"Inner peace begins the moment you choose not to allow another person or event to control your emotions."

PEMA CHODRON, AMERICAN TIBETAN BUDDHIST

* * *

"The light shines in the darkness, and the darkness did not overcome it."

JOHN 1:5

* * *

"The Lord is near to the brokenhearted, and saves the crushed in spirit."

PSALM 34:18

FIFTEEN PRECIOUS MINUTES TO STAKE
OUT SOME PEACEFUL GROUND

Tony Connelly

Peace is an ideal destination, a permanent resolution of conflict between people, friends, family members, countries. Or a temporary absence of noise, strife, stress and work. Peace can also be an opt-out, an evasion from bothersome responsibilities.

Serenity can take a lifetime, and many won't get there. Covering European news, and Brexit, for RTÉ means short- and long-term peace are hard to come by. Deadlines are relentless. Gathering news, rushing to interviews, editing stories for TV, radio, and online all create the kind of over-stimulation that wipes peace off the agenda.

In recent years I've taken up mindfulness to try and stake out some peaceful ground. It's highly intuitive, but it takes effort, or at least commitment. The idea is that our minds get stuck on chatter mode, a persistent inner storyline that may not be all that positive. The chatter can feed upon itself, or get fuelled by incidents, rows, setbacks. If left unchecked, it can develop into anxiety and depression.

Mindfulness doesn't get rid of the chatter, but it trains you to recognise it for what it is. Thoughts are just 'events in the brain' and do not define you or your life. The daily meditation – I try to do 15 minutes every day, sometimes just before a live link on the 9 o'clock news – equips you to step back from the thoughts.

It's grounded in Buddhist meditation but updated by a lot of new science on neuroplasticity, i.e. mindfulness can start to change the chemistry in the brain. Whatever is going on, you focus on the breath, the physical sensations and follow the meditation. Hard to explain, but the mind and the body kind of become fused and in those moments when the storyline gets overwhelming you can call in that sensation, reset, step back and usher in momentary peace.

. . . .

Tony Connelly is a Journalist and Author. He is Europe Editor for RTÉ News and Current Affairs.

*"Success is measured by your
discipline and inner peace."*

MIKE DITKA,
FORMER AMERICAN FOOTBALL PLAYER

* * *

"I hold you in the palm of my hand."

ISAIAH 49:16

* * *

*"Now may the Lord of peace himself give
you peace at all times in all ways.
The Lord be with all of you."*

2 THESSALONIANS 3:16

THE DAY I'M IN

· · · · · · · · · · · · · · · · · · ·

Rita Ann Higgins

I only have today
    so I will try to use it well.
    I will walk on Ballyloughane beach
as I often do.
I will walk to a certain point
and leave my troubles there.
They are invisible
but they can be weighty -
dragging the sap out of my day.

When I walk back
I will feel lighter
and happier.
No one will know, but I will.
I will do the same tomorrow
but tomorrow doesn't count.
I only have this day -
the day I'm in.

· ·

Rita Ann Higgins is a poet and playwright from Galway.

"History says, don't hope
On this side of the grave.
But then, once in a lifetime
The longed-for tidal wave
Of justice can rise up,
And hope and history rhyme."

SEAMUS HEANEY, POET

* * *

"For surely I know the plans I have
for you, says the Lord, plans for your
welfare and not for harm, to give you a
future with hope."

JEREMIAH 29:11

NOT AT PEACE

. . . .

Richard Hendrick

At present I am not at peace.

A million things are zooming through my head, constant lists are being made and remade of all that I have to do, should be doing, and even worse should have done ages ago.

Oh and I've to write this piece too!

There are many things demanding attention and many 'selves' that want to respond in many different ways.

I realise this may not be what you want to read in a book on peace.

But it's true.

At present I am not at peace.

But here's the important bit... that's ok.

It's ok because it is simply how it is with me at present.

And I know, deep down truly know, that if I sit with the present moment as it honestly is, accepting it for what it is and accepting me for my reactions to it, then peace begins to steal in.

This is what prayer and practice have shown me over many years.

Peace is not something to be gained once and held on to forever.

Peace is a practice.

Peace is a choice.

Sometimes it is a very difficult choice, perhaps because the distractions are loud, or because I am pulled into past patterns or future anxieties.

So in these moments of non-peace we find ourselves in what is to be done?

I believe we must surrender to the present moment in its essential truth.

No matter how terrible that may seem, truth is the foundation of peace.

Secondly we must let go of how we would like it to be.

I would like to be at peace right now.

But I'm not.

If I spend my time thinking about how it should be then I will never touch peace.

The conditions for peace can only arise when we open the doors of the heart to reality as it is in all its wonder and even in all its pain.

How we face this reality then becomes important; and so the third step is to greet the now with stillness.

To abide in stillness in the present moment.

To anchor ourselves in its sacred potential as it arises from the Divine.

I am here, now.

All the conditions of my life, known and unknown, helpful and unhelpful have led to this moment.

When I am fully present to it, abiding in it, accepting its potential as grace, then there comes a shift which allows me to choose my reaction to it, to begin to choose peace.

This reaction will not change the present moment one iota.

But it changes me.

In changing me it allows for the gates of possibility to open in this moment, the possibility of growing in awareness, wisdom, compassion and love.

The moment may still be a difficult one.

But there is freedom in the moment to choose my reaction, and I choose peace.

Not peace as a mere cessation of conflict, but the peace that underlies all that is.

The peace promised to us as that which passes all understanding.

The peace that flows with grace.

The peace that changes me so that in me the world too may be changed.

At present I am not at peace.

But I know with truth, with acceptance, and with stillness, peace is possible in this and every moment.

. . . .

Richard Hendrick is a priest-friar of the Irish branch of the Capuchin Franciscan Order.

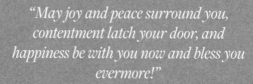

"May joy and peace surround you, contentment latch your door, and happiness be with you now and bless you evermore!"

Irish blessing

* * *

"May there be peace within your walls and security within your citadels."

Psalm 122:7

* * *

"Peace I leave with you; my peace I give to you. I do not give to you as the world gives. Do not let your hearts be troubled, and do not let them be afraid."

John 14:27

IN THE SILENCE BEHIND THE NOISE

Colm Mac Con Iomaire

Peace is always there in the silence behind the noise, but much like the blue sky above the clouds, it's a matter of where we place our attention. In the opening verse of his wonderful poem about a fellow Dubliner – the late great Barney McKenna – poet and fiddler John Sheahan remembers watching Barney give a young banjo player advice on how to hold his plectrum (the piece of plastic you pluck the string with).

'Your plectrum, a fledgling bird;
Squeezed too tightly, it chokes;
Too lightly it flies away.'[1]

It could have been Confucius dispensing pearls on the nature of enlightenment.

Having spent most of my life in music I have come to know the ebb and flow of creativity. The tension that precedes the composition; the static that conjures the lightning. The need to hold on and to let go simultaneously, is a familiar concept. To tighten chokes the melody and to let go makes the melody falls apart. The sweet spot in between is where music lives and flows.

---

1 Banjo Barney from the book *Fiddle Dreams* by John Sheahan, Dedalus Press, 2015.

I recently returned to meditation (via a Zoom course) and I was reminded of that same peaceful vigilance that I know from music. To meditate is to add a keel to your boat; it steadies the ship and makes for smoother sailings in choppy waters.

It's like returning to a home in yourself that you can't believe that you had forgotten.

Imagine for a minute, a school curriculum that introduced young people to their own personal stillness and how transformative that could be for future generations.

A quiet revolution.

. . . .

Dublin born and Wexford-based, Colm Mac Con Iomaire is a well-known violinist, composer, film score arranger, and a founding-member of hugely successful Irish bands The Frames and Kíla.

"Inner peace can be reached only when we practice forgiveness. Forgiveness is letting go of the past, and is therefore the means for correcting our misperceptions."

GERALD G. JAMPOLSKY, PSYCHIATRIST & AUTHOR

* * *

"Be kind to one another, tenderhearted, forgiving one another, as God in Christ has forgiven you."

EPHESIANS 4:32

TUNING INTO MYSELF AND THE WORLD

· ·

John Sheahan

War and peace are words that are often coupled in a list of opposites.

In our troubled, war-torn world, the word 'peace' tends to have a one-dimensional focus – the end of conflict – but peace has wider connotations than the absence of war.

I'm thinking of a personal inner peace, where one is in tune with oneself, at ease with all that enters one's consciousness, in harmony with surroundings and free of conflict.

When our tranquillity is threatened by fear and anxiety, we must develop a technique of addressing these distractions. We might find guidance and inspiration in a prayer by Reinhold Niebuhr:

'Lord grant me the serenity to accept the things I cannot change, the courage to change the things I can, and the wisdom to know the difference.'

Often in life we torment ourselves pondering situations over which we have no control; agonising over predictions which may never materialise.

To live in the moment, free of turmoil, we ought to cultivate the art of entering a silent space where we can reflect on the wonder of our being; survey our progress on the journey between the two great mysteries and develop a deeper awareness of that inner spiritual entity we call the soul, the invisible core of our being.

When I scan my stream of consciousness, and find no major concerns on the landscape of my mind, I feel at peace, in tune with myself and the world around me.

I sense peace and serenity in the reassuring pulse of creation,

The rising and setting of the sun,

The heartbeat of waves caressing a shoreline,

The unwritten symphony of a dawn chorus,

The lament of leaves in a wind-blown forest,

The peaceful face of a sleeping child.

John Sheahan is a musician and composer,
and member of folk group The Dubliners.

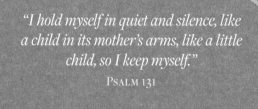

"I hold myself in quiet and silence, like a child in its mother's arms, like a little child, so I keep myself."

PSALM 131

* * *

"We seek peace, knowing that peace is the climate of freedom."

DWIGHT D. EISENHOWER,

FORMER AMERICAN PRESIDENT

* * *

"For freedom Christ has set us free. Stand firm, therefore, and do not submit again to a yoke of slavery."

GALATIANS 5:1

AWAY FROM THE TICKING CLOCK

Olivia O'Leary

I find peace walking beside the Barrow. Yesterday at dusk, there was still light in the sky so it silvered the river even as the woods on either side went dark. That shining ribbon of water tells my life story. All the people I loved who boated and swam in this river are gone before me downstream. The rest of my life and my daughter's life is hidden from me upstream, to be embraced as I embrace the water every year, swimming upriver into the current.

There's no noise, not even my own footfall on the soft grass – just the sound of birds and water. There's no clock – only sun and light tell the time. Getting away from the ticking clock, from the fear of time passing, is essential to finding peace, it seems to me. Only then, absorbed so completely in where we are or what we are doing that we forget time itself, do we feel properly alive.

For centuries pilgrims travelled this river to the blessed well at St Mullins, believed to protect from the plague. Some are said to have travelled onwards to catch the ship at Waterford for La Coruña and the Camino de Santiago. Others used the river to escape, like Eileen Kavanagh from Poulmounty Castle, of the song, 'Eibhlin a Ruin'. It's said that in the 17th century she fled up this river with her lover, Cearbhall O Dalaigh, until they were sheltered by the Abbot of Duiske in Graignamanagh. As the water flows by, there's a real sense of the ancient, and the new.

At dawn and dusk, the wild things come out. I watch those ripples near the bank and soon I'll see an otter surface. Stoats with their young dart back into the bushes and peer out to see if I'm still there. As I head home in the evening, I'll often be startled by an owl flying low over my head.

I'm at home with nature, with myself. I'm at peace.

. . . .

Olivia O'Leary has presented current affairs programmes for the last three decades for RTÉ, BBC and ITV. As a print journalist, she has written about politics for both the Sunday Tribune *and the* Irish Times. *She is the presenter of RTÉ Radio 1's* The Poetry Programme.

"The more freedom we enjoy, the greater the responsibility we bear, toward others as well as ourselves."

OSCAR ARIAS SANCHEZ,
COSTA RICAN ACTIVIST &
NOBEL PEACE PRIZE LAUREATE

* * *

"Love your enemies, do good to those who hate you, speak well of those who speak badly of you, pray for those mistreat you."

LUKE 6:27-28

THE SEAT OF PEACE

. . . .

Paul Muldoon

It was in Dublin, as it happens, that the quantum physicist Erwin Schrödinger proposed that when his equations seemed to present differing histories, these were 'not alternatives, but all really happen simultaneously'. This theory is sometimes known as 'superposition', and is based on the idea that quantum particles may exist in different states at the same time.

The notion of something akin to a parallel universe has been a feature of the Celtic mindset for millennia and holds sway today. Even now, no country dweller would dream of cutting down a fairy thorn lest it upset the balance of things.

What keeps the balance between this world and the next intact is our belief in it. It's no accident that the fairy folk are known in Irish as the aes sidhe, 'the people of peace'. Another, related, Irish term for peace is síocháin, which refers to the state of being calm or untroubled. We see it in the term for the peace-keeping police force, An Garda Síochána.

There's an etymological connection, through their common Indo-European roots, between the Irish words sidhe and síocháin and the English words seat, sit and settle. The 'seats' of the fairy folk are their fairy mounds, from which they are indivisible. The mounds themselves are 'sites' or 'settlements' in the earth.

One of the most striking images in Irish literature comes from Acallam na Senórach, the great conversation between Caoilte, Oisín and St Patrick about the old and new ways; it involves a fawn that's chased by the Fianna until it suddenly disappears into what turns out to be a fairy fort.

It's for this reason that, if I feel disquieted, I imagine myself as a fawn (sometimes an eilit mhaol or hornless doe), slipping into the side of a hill, through a 'thin' point between realms. I imagine myself slipping into a tumulus grave from which, in one intellection, the stone has been rolled away.

. . . .

Paul Muldoon is a poet and professor of poetry, as well as an editor, critic, playwright, lyricist and translator.

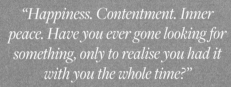

"Happiness. Contentment. Inner peace. Have you ever gone looking for something, only to realise you had it with you the whole time?"

ANONYMOUS

* * *

"Contemplation is listening to the silence of God."

THOMAS MERTON, AMERICAN TRAPPIST MONK, POET AND MYSTIC.

* * *

"This is the day that the LORD has made; let us rejoice and be glad in it."

PSALMS 118:24

IF I WERE PEACE

Anne Maire Maguire

I
f I were Peace,
    I would yield like frosted landscape to the morning sun
    I would burst forth like a new year snowdrop
I would snooze like a full-bellied cat in summer
I would let fresh winds blow the cobwebs away
And sit with the sun on my back.

I would meet with the Hawthorn and Elder
I would heed the Robin's counsel
I would watch the Heron, unmoving in storm water
I would see what the Fox had to say about all this.

If I were Peace,
I would sing full-voiced into the valley below
I would talk, I would listen, I would hear
I would celebrate,
I would worry, I would grieve, I would comfort
I would close my eyes in horror
I would ask for help, I would offer help

I would let delight move uninhibited through me
I would thank
I would pray.

If I were Peace,
I would reveal, I would shine
I would seek shelter
I would expand, I would try, I would risk
I would wait
I would fail, I would fall, I would fight
I would run away, I would stop
I would succumb, I would overcome
I would fall to my knees in relief
I would let it go.

If I were Peace, I would remind myself to abide here
I would be Still, I would rest, I would quieten
I would forgive all that I do in the name of Peace
I would forgive my humanity
I would forgive all humanity
I would withdraw from the tides of Life
From the comings, the goings, the ebbing and flowing
And return instead to the innerscape of Peace
Here, I would let the creature rest
Here, I would drop anchor.

Anne Marie Maguire is a T'ai Chi and Qigong instructor, herbalist and naturopath, with special interests in the mystical traditions, energetics and the healing power of nature. She currently teaches T'ai Chi and Qigong, with a focus on healing, meditation and spirituality. She is the author of Hidden Contemplatives and a lay Associate of St Mary's Abbey, Glencairn, Co. Waterford.

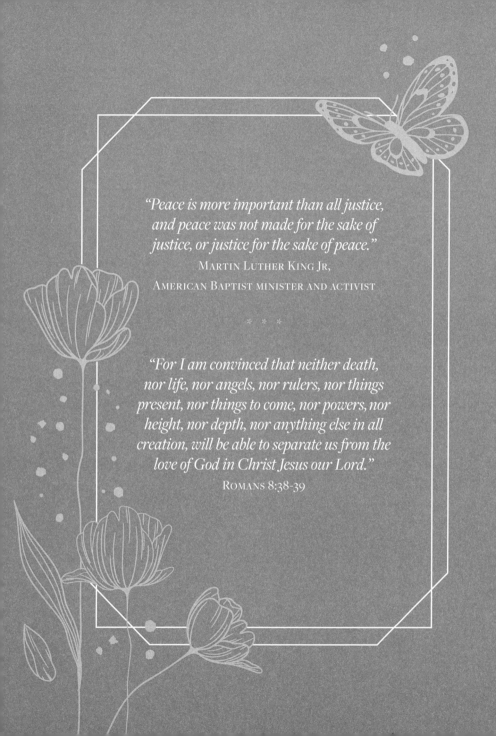

"Peace is more important than all justice, and peace was not made for the sake of justice, or justice for the sake of peace."

MARTIN LUTHER KING JR,
AMERICAN BAPTIST MINISTER AND ACTIVIST

* * *

"For I am convinced that neither death, nor life, nor angels, nor rulers, nor things present, nor things to come, nor powers, nor height, nor depth, nor anything else in all creation, will be able to separate us from the love of God in Christ Jesus our Lord."

ROMANS 8:38-39

TORAH AND TRANQUILLITY

Rabbi Zalman Lent

'*odeh Ani* – Thank You' are the very first two words of a
Jewish prayer uttered in the morning, whispered literally
as soon as we open our eyes after a night's sleep: 'Thank
you, living and eternal King, for mercifully restoring my soul, your
faithfulness is great.'

That short sentence, just 12 words in the original Hebrew, is the first
part of a two-part ancient Jewish recipe for finding peace in our daily lives.

It reminds us, before any of the upcoming day's joys and stresses
even percolate into our sleepy heads, that we must be grateful to simply
be alive for another day. If we are still breathing then it means we are
needed here on Earth, we have a mission to fulfil – we are important to
the Creator.

Once we have expressed, and felt, true gratitude then the rest of the
day falls into a correct perspective. Extreme emotions of joy or sorrow
are tempered by the knowledge that life is granted to us one day at a time,
and we are never entirely sure which one is our last. Every day needs to
be made worthwhile, filled with achievement.

The day closes with an important prayer too, Ribono Shel Olam –
Master of the Universe. In this paragraph we undertake to forgive anyone
who has harmed us in the course of the day, '...anyone who has angered,

antagonised or sinned against me'. This allows us to fall asleep with a clear heart and mind, free of the burdens which keep so many awake – who bothered me today, who disrespected me today, who took what was mine today, etc.

It may not be easy, and it may not even be possible to fully forgive everyone each night – but those who are able to wield that superpower of forgiveness easily can truly sleep the sleep of the righteous.

With a day full of gratitude, and a night full of forgiveness, how can we not live a life of inner peace?

. . . .

Rabbi Zalman Lent leads the Orthodox Jewish Community in Dublin.

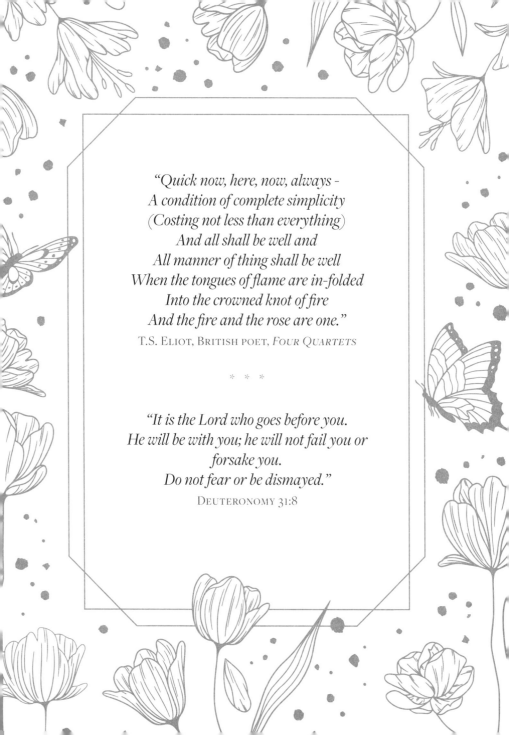

"*Quick now, here, now, always -*
A condition of complete simplicity
(Costing not less than everything)
And all shall be well and
All manner of thing shall be well
When the tongues of flame are in-folded
Into the crowned knot of fire
And the fire and the rose are one."

T.S. ELIOT, BRITISH POET, *FOUR QUARTETS*

* * *

"*It is the Lord who goes before you.*
He will be with you; he will not fail you or
forsake you.
Do not fear or be dismayed."

DEUTERONOMY 31:8

ALL WILL BE WELL AND ALL MANNER
OF THINGS WILL BE WELL

Eamon Ryan

I'm the product of two people, my mother and my father. Both have given me advice over the years that helps me find peace in a busy, mad, hectic world.

My father, who died four years ago, was quite a philosophical, spiritual person, who had an almost Buddha-like ability to retain his good humour even in difficult times.

He would have always advocated that you take occasional 10 minute breaks to centre yourself; that's the way he described it. It doesn't have to be in a darkened room with a candle burning. It can be anywhere, even on your way from A to B, to rest your mind, and rest yourself.

I would add to that an outlook, a kind of spiritual sense of wonder about being in the world, and ultimately listening to that advice of Julian of Norwich, that 'All will be well, all will be well, and all manner of things will be well', that things will work out.

My mother is a very different person, but she said something to me once and it really struck home. You have to remember that a person you are dealing with might have a 'stone in their shoe', something that's really bothering them, that can influence why they may seem so put out or difficult.

That sounds so obvious, but it's a really simple lesson: put yourself in the other's person's shoes. If you come towards people in that way, it is actually a great liberation for yourself, as it makes it easier not to get anxious or stressed if things are not going exactly the way you want.

Being forgiving of yourself can sound like a get-out clause for all your failings, but I think it's key to be able to do the other two things; to be a little bit kind to yourself.

Being able to centre yourself, being in the moment, being mindful of what another person's troubles might be, and being forgiving of yourself; that's what I try to do to keep a sense of peace.

. . . .

Eamon Ryan TD is the Minister for Environment, Climate, Communications and Transport, and leader of the Green Party. Before entering politics he ran a cycling tourism business. He lives in Dublin and is married with four children.

"All we are saying, is give peace a chance."

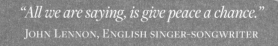

John Lennon, English singer-songwriter

* * *

"For a child has been born for us,
a son given to us;
authority rests upon his shoulders;
and he is named
Wonderful Counselor, Mighty God,
Everlasting Father, Prince of Peace."

Isaiah 9:6

* * *

"In everything do to others as you would
have them do to you; for this is the law
and the prophets."

Matthew 7:12

SOUL CYCLES

· · · · · · · · · · · · · · · · ·

Roisin Ingle

I've been looking for peace my entire life. Hasn't everyone? I've searched for it on ten-day silent meditation retreats, where you rise at 4am, sit cross-legged in a hall for hours and have your last meal of the day before noon. I've looked for it in the chipper, where, for a few transcendent moments a batter burger offers respite from what ails you, before what ails you returns with a bang and a side order of shame.

I've searched for tranquillity on Indian mountain tops and in a bottle of wine and once, on Inis Oirr, I found it for five minutes while swimming with my daughters in the clearest waters near a dolphin. I've searched for peace walking the Great South Wall or reading a good book or cradling newborn twin girls in my arms or singing folk songs with friends. I've sought it out in my partner's eyes and in a West of Ireland sunset and in a deserted pandemic Dublin town and on a website where everything was 70% off.

I find peace sometimes. But it's fleeting, like the robin that visits my garden wall and never stays long enough for a proper chat. When I need guaranteed, longer-lasting peace I make my excuses to my family and get on my bike. I point it towards the Royal Canal Greenway. I fly past water and people pushing buggies and traffic and Luke Kelly's head and across the bridge named for Samuel Beckett and on through the glowing red sticks and on and on and on. Cycling calms me down, straightens me out, plants me in the now, fires my creativity, and eases the turbulence in my mind, body and soul. My bike is a teacher with one lesson: if you move towards peace you will get there. In the end.

Roisin Ingle is an Irish Times *columnist and co-producer of* The Women's Podcast *on irishtimes.com. She is the author of two collections of her columns* Pieces of Me *and* Public Displays of Emotion *and co-author, with Natasha Fennell, of* The Daughterhood.

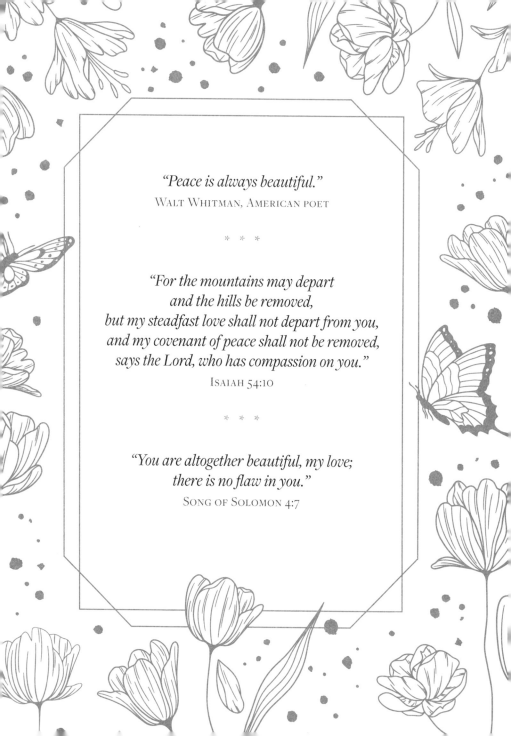

"Peace is always beautiful."

WALT WHITMAN, AMERICAN POET

* * *

"For the mountains may depart
and the hills be removed,
but my steadfast love shall not depart from you,
and my covenant of peace shall not be removed,
says the Lord, who has compassion on you."

ISAIAH 54:10

* * *

"You are altogether beautiful, my love;
there is no flaw in you."

SONG OF SOLOMON 4:7

INNER STILLNESS

. . . .

Dag Hammarskjöld

Peace comes from making time for moments of quiet and stillness in our day. When Dag Hammarskjöld was head of the United Nations he established a meditation room in the headquarters in New York to give diplomats, employees and visitors – regardless of religion – the opportunity to retreat for prayer, meditation and quiet time.

He wrote an inspirational text in his own hand and placed it in the room. The first sentence of the text read 'in each of us there is a centre of stillness surrounded by silence'. By this inner stillness he probably meant what the mystics call 'the fine tip of the soul'. He rightly knew that this stillness exists already in each of us; we do not need to create it. What we need to do is to find the spot where it can be accessed.

The path may have been travelled very little by us or it may have been overgrown, but it is there if we seek it. 'Be still and know that I am God,' the psalmist sings.

. . . .

Dag Hammarskjöld was a Swedish economist and diplomat who served as the second Secretary-General of the United Nations in 1953 for a five-year term and was re-elected in 1957. He died in an air cash in 1961 and was awarded the Nobel Peace Prize posthumously that year.

"The quieter you become,
The more you can hear."

RAM DASS, SPIRITUAL TEACHER & PSYCHOLOGIST

* * *

"For the mountains may depart
and the hills be removed,
but my steadfast love shall not depart from you,
and my covenant of peace shall not be removed,
says the Lord, who has compassion on you."

ISAIAH 54:10

* * *

"For God alone my soul waits in silence,
for my hope is from him."

PSALM 62:5

THE TRANQUILLITY OF A TANTRUM

Fiona Sherlock

The flushed cheeks of a quietly dozing child, their little chest puffing with small sleepy breaths – well to observe this is the epitome of peace. But harmony is also there in other not so peaceful settings. It's in the angry cry of an overtired infant searching for relief, or the squealing tantrum of a toddler who does not want to leave. It's not obvious, in those moments. But I can just about see it, from the corner of my eye. Like a novel in the bookshelf, peace can be accessed easily once you notice it is there.

When on the front line of soothing a roaring baby, I have a conversation with 80-year-old me. I may be drenched in sweat and milk, she on a rocking chair by the fire. She slides varifocals down her nose and asks me to sniff his hair, or stroke his pudgy wrist, to take in his pure perfection and babyhood. She brings me peace, reminding me that time will march on. That he will stop crying soon. And one day, he will be too big for my arms, for my house.

For me, peace comes in being in the moment, but not of the moment. It is choosing to stay calm and breathe deeply when the child needs peace from you more than anything else. It is being resigned to rocking or just being there to give a hug when the tantrum lulls and one is wanted.

If these loud and disruptive moments did not exist, then neither would the calm and quiet ones. A yawn of tired satisfaction arrives at the end of the day, once the children are snoozing. But it wouldn't mean anything without the wild moments, because peace and conflict exist together, like day and night or yin and yang. It is in diffusing the difficult times with calm, that it comes at me, like a soothing bullet.

. . . .

Fiona Sherlock is a writer and mother of two from Bective, Co. Meath. She is the author of Twelve Motives for Murder *and also creates virtual mystery games, writes poetry and occasionally columns for the* Sunday Independent.

"We who lived in concentration camps
can remember the men who walked
through the huts comforting others,
giving away their last piece of bread.
They may have been few in number,
but they offer sufficient proof that
everything can be taken from a man
but one thing: the last of the human
freedoms – to choose one's attitude
in any given set of circumstances, to
choose one's own way."

Victor Franklin,
neurologist & Holocaust survivor

QUIET IN THE MIDST OF NOISE

Marty Whelan

Peace and how you find it. Now, there's a tall order in a world of constant hustle and bustle, or at least that's been the world we remember prior to March 2020. Peace – free from disturbance, tranquillity. Finding calm and releasing stress – oh the joy.

In my normal world of morning radio on Lyric FM and *Winning Streak* on RTÉ television, there are moments of peace. But you've got to be vigilant in finding those moments. I am very conscious of picking certain pieces of music or songs at breakfast so the listener and I can share moments of calm in the waking hours. The music of Ennio Morricone, Debussy, opera from Puccini's 'La Boheme', the quiet gentleness of 'Hymns to the Silence' by Van Morrison, in fact, any of Van's gentler songs invites meditation and contemplation.

In TV it's difficult as there are so many involved and it's always a group event. But quiet moments, by myself in my dressing room, can often afford me the space to zone out of the world around me and just be. If only for a few minutes. Sister Stan speaks of listening to your breathing. I try that, it works but only when I can just be and there's no call on me from anywhere else.

Perhaps it's being an only child, but I find solitude easy. Silence doesn't unnerve me or the absence of company make me lunge for the phone. I was blessed with loving parents and am surrounded by love at home with Maria and our two adult children, Jessica and Thomas – our closeness brings its own sense of peace.

Reading is a great source of peace too. Sitting on my favourite seat, watching the murmuration of the birds over the trees at the back of our house. It reminds me of my mam's advice when I was a little boy; she would say, 'When you see the birds going home, it's time for you to come home too'.

Peace is sometimes found on a sunny day walking the grounds of Malahide Castle or on Portmarnock Beach. Perhaps, staring at a full moon (Mrs Whelan's great passion) and feeling tiny and part of an immense universe. It can also come from having an early night, thinking of the good that happened in the day, and drifting off.

God has his part to play and those conversations always bring a feeling of peace. Quiet contemplation, sometimes in the midst of noise, is possible – keeping calm, that's the thing. Now, let's put on Van Morrison singing the song 'In the Garden' and let the peace wash over us.

. . . .

Marty Whelan is an award-winning radio and television broadcaster.

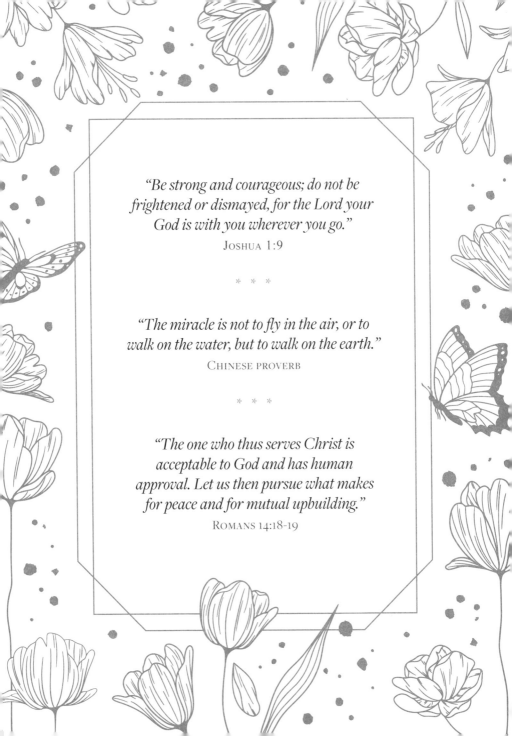

"Be strong and courageous; do not be frightened or dismayed, for the Lord your God is with you wherever you go."

JOSHUA 1:9

* * *

"The miracle is not to fly in the air, or to walk on the water, but to walk on the earth."

CHINESE PROVERB

* * *

"The one who thus serves Christ is acceptable to God and has human approval. Let us then pursue what makes for peace and for mutual upbuilding."

ROMANS 14:18-19

THE BUSINESS OF PEACE

Danny McCoy

Peace for me is found in having purpose in both family life and business life. If peace is an absence of conflict, then finding a good work/life balance is the key. I don't consider my home life and my work to be strictly distinct but rather blended; probably as a result of being fortunate to have a family that I love and enjoy being with, and a job that I am absorbed by and find fulfilling.

Moments that I find peaceful are in the weekend freedom to go for a walk with my wife or take a solitary run with no fixed intended route on starting out, but just following the roads and back-lanes of the city as my curiosity encourages me.

Less frequently, strumming a ukulele for my own pleasure and the patient tolerance of others is another source of peace; for me at least. When the weather is favourable I like to sit on a favourite chair in the garden to read or to catch up on work emails, but very rarely just to think. I still marvel at the technology of the tablet computer and it's my constant fixture which opens up endless opportunities for nostalgia and wonderment, and which gives me amusement and solace.

I enjoy talk show radio, necessary for work but also out of interest. I really enjoy getting to sit on the couch at night to watch TV with Ailish and whilst I'm mostly complaining about what's on, it's still a peaceful way to end the day.

. . . .

Danny McCoy is the CEO of IBEC, Ireland's largest lobby and business representative group.

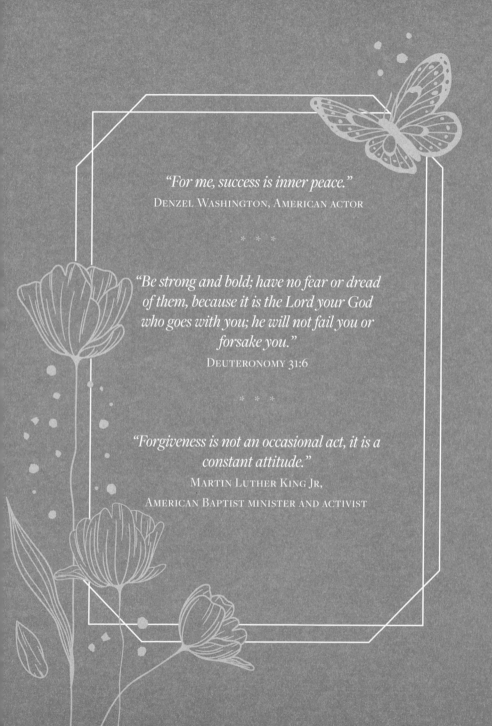

"For me, success is inner peace."

DENZEL WASHINGTON, AMERICAN ACTOR

* * *

*"Be strong and bold; have no fear or dread
of them, because it is the Lord your God
who goes with you; he will not fail you or
forsake you."*

DEUTERONOMY 31:6

* * *

*"Forgiveness is not an occasional act, it is a
constant attitude."*

MARTIN LUTHER KING JR,
AMERICAN BAPTIST MINISTER AND ACTIVIST

WHERE I FIND PEACE IN MY LIFE

Sr Bernadine Meskill

As postulants and novices, we were regularly told that 'peace is the tranquillity of order'. At that stage our Novice Mistress was waging a battle, in vain, to get us raw recruits to keep our rooms and our work places tidy. Now, some 57 years down the line, I know from experience that peace IS the tranquillity of order, but now I realise that it involves far more than keeping rooms tidy!

In all our lives there are circumstances that upset and disturb us emotionally and mentally, and can even shatter our peace. Personally, I find that I can only have real and deep peace if I listen to my heart. When I turn to God in the depth of my heart and there let my thoughts and memories roam around on the goodness and grace that has saved me from myself and held me safely in spite of fear and foreboding... then I know that 'all will be well'.

Some people imagine that in an enclosed order like ours there are skies without storms, work without fatigue, relationships without disappointments. Far from it. We carry the 'human condition' like everyone else, but we have learned that 'forgiveness is a funny thing; it warms the heart and cools the sting'. When we read the Psalms, we are told that 'peace is the seed-ground of holiness' and so it is.

In my life, I am very blessed to have true friends, both inside and outside the cloister, who have very wise and listening ears when I need a stabilising influence on the shifting sands of my emotions. I thank God that I am so blessed. They give me both spiritual and practical advice, and are real channels of peace in my life. Someone told me lately, when I was going through a stressful time, that I should just shut the drawer on my worry and not open it until I was ready to handle it. As novices we would have been told to 'place it in the hands of God' – an example of spiritual and practical advice, and both work well.

I have a very simple prayer 'Sacred Heart of Jesus I place all my trust in you', which I have been saying – breathing – a million times a day since I was a child. No matter what the crisis, that little prayer brings me peace.

And then there are my doves – well they are pigeons, but to me they are beautiful doves. All my worries float away on the wings of my doves. The minute I go out the door, down they flock and I don't have a worry in the world as I enjoy watching them billing and cooing.

Sr Bernadine Meskill is the Abbess of the Poor Clares Monastery in Ennis, Co. Clare.

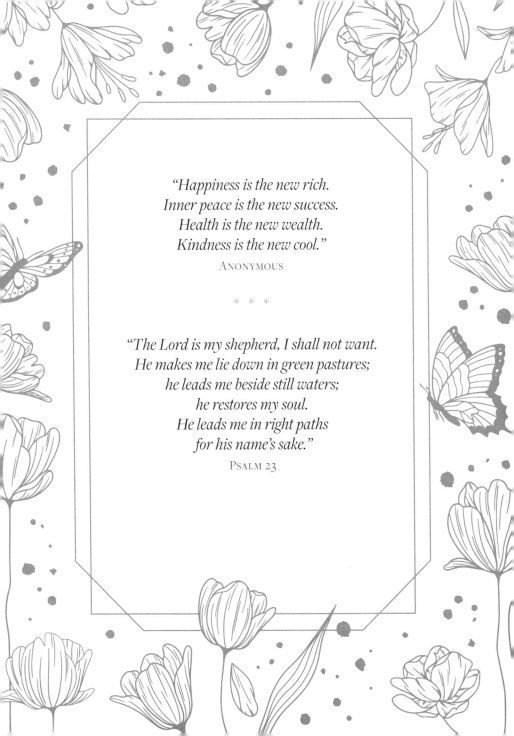

*"Happiness is the new rich.
Inner peace is the new success.
Health is the new wealth.
Kindness is the new cool."*

ANONYMOUS

* * *

*"The Lord is my shepherd, I shall not want.
He makes me lie down in green pastures;
he leads me beside still waters;
he restores my soul.
He leads me in right paths
for his name's sake."*

PSALM 23

THE MUSIC OF THE UNIVERSE

Ian Robertson

A mindfulness app that I use gives an interesting exercise to help find peace amidst the whizzing thoughts that often fill my mind. The instructor tells me to pay attention to the space between my thoughts. So I tried that. It worked the first time because it put the thoughts in perspective. I sat back and watched them the way I have done sometimes when on holiday, watching the busy commuters rushing for their trains at some Italian rush-hour station. I enjoyed the luxury of just watching while sipping my cappuccino and this detached, relaxed, peaceful perspective made me want to call out to the commuters – and my thoughts – hey, slow down, there are incredible things around you.

And the most incredible of these is that mysterious gap between the thoughts. It's a bit like the spaces between Beethoven's notes – these exquisite moments of silence without which the beauty of his music would evaporate. When I focus my attention on this backdrop, it doesn't diminish either the music or the thoughts. Instead, it triggers in me a sort of peaceful compassion for their fragility. The next note or thought are each a transitory vibration against the backcloth of eternity.

When the TV is mis-tuned between stations you see a mush of static interference. But a proportion of that confusion of signal is actually caused by cosmic background radiation, going back to the beginning of the universe, the Big Bang, 13.7 billion years ago. Sometimes when I tune into the space between thoughts, I fancy that I, like the TV, can detect a sort of eternal hum that is as timeless as this background radiation.

No, let me call it the music of the universe, as endlessly beautiful as it is peaceful.

. . . .

Ian Robertson is a clinical psychologist and neuroscientist. Currently he is co-director of the Global Brain Health Institute and Emeritus Professor at Trinity College Dublin. He is widely recognised as one of the world's leading researchers in neuropsychology.

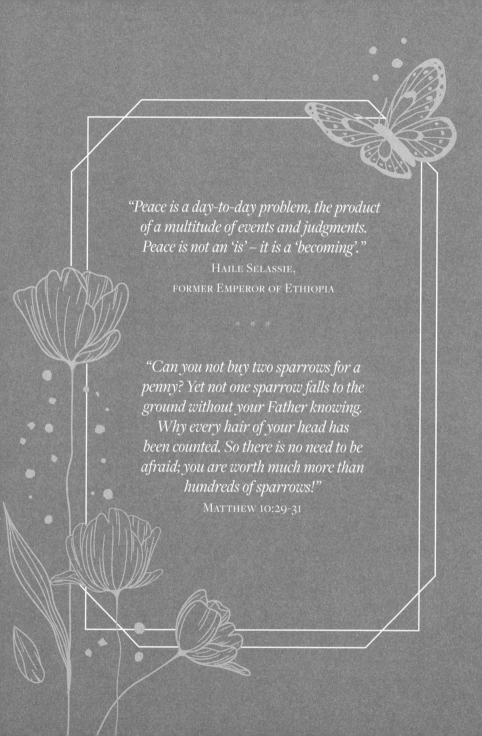

*"Peace is a day-to-day problem, the product
of a multitude of events and judgments.
Peace is not an 'is' – it is a 'becoming'."*

HAILE SELASSIE,
FORMER EMPEROR OF ETHIOPIA

∗ ∗ ∗

*"Can you not buy two sparrows for a
penny? Yet not one sparrow falls to the
ground without your Father knowing.
Why every hair of your head has
been counted. So there is no need to be
afraid; you are worth much more than
hundreds of sparrows!"*

MATTHEW 10:29-31

PEACE IS TOGETHERNESS

Mary Lou MacDonald

There is an old Irish saying, '*Ar scáth a chéile a mhaireann na daoine*'. It carries the meaning '*in the shelter of each other's shadows, the people live*'. When we think of peace we often think of the absence of conflict but peace is truly found in the presence of togetherness and in the fellowship of our shared experience and understanding. I have always felt most at peace when part of something that is bigger than myself – things that transcend my individual needs, challenges and worries. Family, friends and community are the things that sustain us in good times and bad. To step out of the door in the morning and feel truly connected to a wider world is incredibly uplifting. To belong, to be amongst others, to be there for others and for them to be there for me in return is to touch the very pulsing heart of life.

I have been in big rooms for big meetings. However, when I reflect on the times that bring me peace and fulfilment, I see a tapestry of simple, precious moments. Moments shared with my husband and children, chats with friends where we shoot the breeze and put the world to right over a cup of tea and treasured phone calls with my mum Joan, in which she keeps my feet firmly on the ground while also rekindling my confidence and determination to take the next steps in the journey of life. I recall times of anxiety when I have stood in my driveway in the early light of dawn, taken a deep breath and listened to the sounds of a slumbering Cabra waking to the prospect of a new day. To bear witness to the chorus of community life is a privilege I never take for granted. Being surrounded by a loving family, a strong community and good neighbours has provided me with a deep reservoir of strength. To know that I can always come back to this place where I belong is a powerful, inspiring feeling. Community is my peace. Belonging is my peace. Home is my peace.

Living in the shelter of one another is how we have gotten through some very dark times over the past year. As the storm has raged around our boat, every simple act of kindness has brought us closer to shore. We have relied on each other, depended on each other, and shown-up for each other. That we have lived the meaning of the proverb 'Ni neart go cur le chéile' gives me great hope that we can build a better, fairer future. By acting together, we can bring a meaningful, everyday sense of peace to those in our society who feel lost, excluded or disadvantaged. That means good jobs, decent homes and a strong safety net to catch us if we fall. When all is said and done, life is all about the search for peace. It is the greatest gift to be at peace with yourself when you lay your head on the pillow at night. It is a gift we should want for everyone.

Mary Lou McDonald is leader of Sinn Féin
and TD for Dublin Central.

'When thoughts become silent, the soul
finds peace in its own source.'
UPANISHADS, THE PHILOSOPHICAL-RELIGIOUS
TEXTS OF HINDUISM

* * *

"Let all that you do be done in love."
1 CORINTHIANS 16:14

* * *

'May there be peace within your walls and
security within your citadels.'
PSALM 122:7

ELUSIVE PEACE

. . . .

Ray D'Arcy

I t won't come as a surprise to the person who told me I wasn't suited to meditation that my mother used to call me the 'Tasmanian Dust Devil' when I was a boy. I've always been active. I've worked since I was nine. I feel a definite guilt if I'm not being productive. So where do I get peace? I don't know. I don't know what peace is. I can tell you this: when I run, I feel at ease. When I run, I can empty my head of the chattering monkeys. Activities that demand my full attention allow me to have some sort of peace or maybe it's just distraction. When I bake brown bread on Saturday mornings, I feel calm as I'm transported back to my Granny's kitchen, where as a boy I observed her doing exactly the same thing. My favourite thing now is a hug from a loved one.

I honestly don't know a world without worry. I don't suffer from anxiety, I'm lucky in that regard, but I am a worrier. I worry therefore I am. I'm jealous of people who can meditate, people who can find peace. I think for some of us silencing our thoughts isn't an option and in trying to do so we just create more hassle for ourselves; or maybe it is that I haven't been doing it properly. I hope you find peace or whatever it is you need to get through this crazy world we live in. Mind yourself. That's important.

. . . .

Ray D'Arcy is a husband, father of two and a broadcaster.

"What life can compare to this? Sitting quietly by the window, I watch the leaves fall and the flowers bloom, as the seasons come and go."

HSUEH-TOU, CHINESE BUDDHIST MONK & POET

* * *

"And the peace of God, which transcends all understanding, will guard your hearts and your minds in Christ Jesus."

PHILIPPIANS 4:7

PEACE IS A CHOICE

Peace is a choice. When it taps me on the shoulder, it takes a turning towards; a gentle acknowledgment; a surrender into its grace. You see, its call can go unnoticed. More often than not, there is a noisier option. Some grief, some problem, a clatter of commotion gnawing at me, pulling me away as it brushes up against me. So, peace is a choice that not only needs to be heard but needs deep commitment.

It can be fleeting: the crackle of a fire, the warmth of a bath or the relaxed gaze on a soft, expansive horizon. It slips in when I am not looking. If I blink, I might miss it. If I don't choose to honour it, if I don't choose to surrender to it, it will pass me by.

However, sometimes I go looking for it.

When I first moved to Ireland from Canada, there was a constant internal struggle to settle. I missed my family, my homeland and all that was familiar. At times, it felt like the world was tightening its grip around me. Indeed, at times it still does. When this happens, I like to head out into nature and touch in with that which is bigger than me: the forests of Wicklow. By noticing all the minutia and the intricate ecosystems that carry on regardless of my egocentric fixations, I realise that there is comfort in the consistency of the natural world. There is peace in the softened footstep on a forest floor, the feeling of air on skin and the wide-open sky.

Once peace arrives, I try my hardest to let it settle into my bones and to feel its sacred embrace. Moreover, like any cherished guest, I welcome peace and give it the space it deserves.

Jane Negrych is the Managing Director of The Sanctuary. She has completed a MSc: Studies in Mindfulness with The University of Aberdeen and is an Honorary Lecturer on the programme. She also teaches on the Caring for the Caregivers programme, the SWAY Programme and the MBLC: Being Present Teacher Training for The Sanctuary.

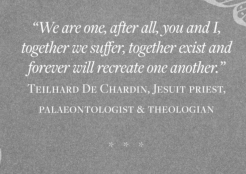

*"We are one, after all, you and I,
together we suffer, together exist and
forever will recreate one another."*

TEILHARD DE CHARDIN, JESUIT PRIEST,
PALAEONTOLOGIST & THEOLOGIAN

* * *

*"What does the Lord require of you but to
do justice, and to love kindness,
and to walk humbly with your God?"*

MICAH 6:8

* * *

*"Peace cannot be kept by force it can only be
achieved by understanding."*

MARTIN LUTHER KING JR, AMERICAN
BAPTIST MINISTER AND ACTIVIST

A WAY OF STOPPING

Nelson Mandela

I n Nelson Mandela's autobiography *The Long Walk to Freedom*, he describes a daily march he endured during his time in prison in South Africa. He wrote: 'it is a 20 minute march from your cramped gloomy prison cell to the limestone quarry. Once there you will slave away with your pick shovel under the searing sun. Your hands blistered and bleeding, your body drenched with sweat and plastered with dust. How would you feel if you were on that march, knowing what lay in store for you?'[2]

However, in the book he calls this march 'a tonic'. For 13 years in Robin Island Prison he marched every single morning, and as he did so he engaged fully with the experience. He noticed the birds flying gracefully through the sky, the cool caress of the wind blowing in from the sea and the fresh smell of the eucalyptus blossoms. He wasn't lost in thought about the hard work that lay ahead of him or the miserable days that lay behind him. He was living fully in the present moment.

Nelson Mandela was a South African anti-apartheid revolutionary, political leader and philanthropist. He sent 27 years as a political prisoner and went on to serve as President of South Africa from 1994 to 1999. He died in 2013.

2   Nelson Mandela, *The Long Walk to Freedom*, Little Brown & Co., 1994.

"Each person deserves a day away in which no problems are confronted, no solutions searched for. Each of us needs to withdraw from the cares which will not withdraw from us."

MAYA ANGELOU,
AMERICAN POET & CIVIL RIGHTS ACTIVIST

* * *

"Speak out for those who cannot speak, for the rights of all the destitute. Speak out, judge righteously, defend the rights of the poor and needy."

PROVERBS 31:6-9

STEPS TOWARDS INNER PEACE

. . . .

Peace Pilgrim

'To attain inner peace you must actually give your life, not just your possessions. When you at last give your life – bringing into alignment your beliefs and the way you live, then, only then, can you begin to find inner peace.'

'The simplification of life is one of the steps to inner peace. A persistent simplification will create an inner and outer well-being that places harmony in one's life.'

'In this world you are given as you give.'

'Only insofar as we remain in harmony with divine law – do good things come to us.'

'When you find peace within yourself, you become the kind of person who can live at peace with others.'

'If you realised how powerful your thoughts are, you would never think a negative thought.'

. . . .

Extracts from the writings of Peace Pilgrim – born Mildred Lisette Norman, she was an American pacifist, vegetarian and peace activist. Starting on January 1, 1953 in Pasadena, California, she adopted the name 'Peace Pilgrim' and walked across the United States for 28 years promoting peace.

CONCURRENCE

"Each day's terror, almost
a form of boredom – madmen
at the wheel and
stepping on the gas and
the brakes no good -
and each day one,
sometimes two, morning-glories,
faultless, blue, blue sometimes
flecked with magenta, each
lit from within with
the first sunlight."[3]

DENISE LEVERTOV, AMERICAN POET

3. Denise Levertov, *Candles in Babylon*,
New Directions Books, 1982.

ACKNOWLEDGEMENTS

I would like to express my appreciation and gratitude to all the people who contributed to this book and who responded with such honesty and openness. A special thanks to my publisher Columba Books and to Garry O'Sullivan for his great support. Much gratitude goes to my editor Mags Gargan and to Alba Esteban for her beautiful design and artwork. Thanks also to Johanne Farrelly for her help and support preparing various drafts of the book.

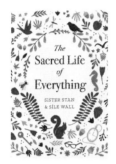

Sacred Life of Everything

ISBN 9781178218365 COLUMBA BOOKS, HARDBACK, 14.99€

Tapping into the everyday moments that can be precious and awe-inspiring, this book full of meditations, prayers and poems is designed to give you a greater sense of presence and inner peace. Filled with images to concentrate your meditations on the beauty of nature and the small grace-filled moments, this is your key to awaken your senses to the wonder of each minute.

Awakening Inner Peace. A Little Book of Hours

ISBN 9781178218344O COLUMBA BOOKS, HARDBACK, 12.99€

Designed for a reader who wants to escape the stresses of everyday life, this modern book of hours is the perfect antidote, providing readers with short, inspiring prayers, poems and biblical quotes they can turn to whenever they need a quiet moment. The book is structured around the traditional monastic schedule of daily prayer and full of prayers designed to be read at any time, by anyone who seeks a moment of peace and connection with God.

Mindful Meditations for Every Day

ISBN 9781178218309O COLUMBA BOOKS, HARDBACK, 12.99€

In this gem of a book, Sr Stan composes meditations and reflections based on her own life. *Mindful Meditations for Every Day* carries the reader through the calendar year, with daily meditations, mindfulness exercises and a new scripture each month. This book teaches the art of being aware, present and grounded. By learning how to focus and be mindful of simple things, such as the breath or the senses, the reader will learn how to relax and simply be in the present moment.

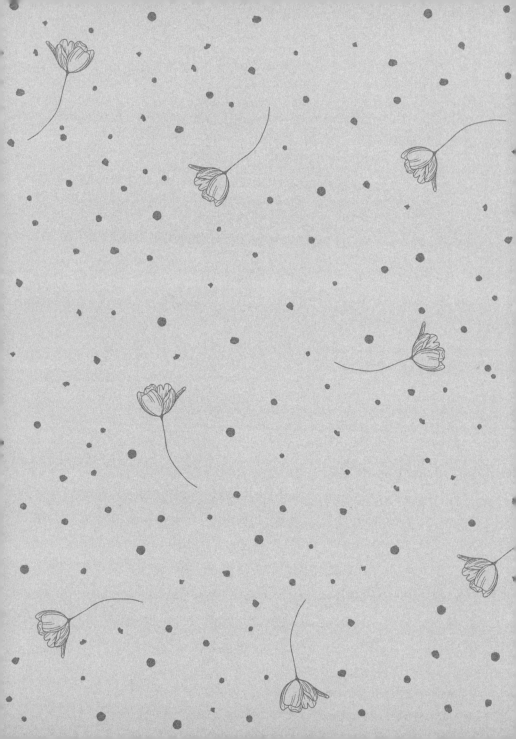